PRAISE FOR *4 GLOBAL CRISES*

"Timely, relevant, profound, this in-depth analysis on the four global challenges could not have emerged at a better time—or by a more qualified writer. Dr. David Ryback's experience as a psychologist, a prolific writer, and an expert on emotional intelligence, provides the exact backdrop for a serious consideration of the issue of survival in today's world. There is no book out there like this—certainly, nothing so comprehensive, so timely. From beginning to end, this book will hold the reader's attention, transforming helpless feelings to greater self-confidence."

—Dr. D. A. Simpson, Professor Emeritus, New Mexico Highlands University

"Easy and enjoyable reading, this book provides concrete guidelines, leading us toward more comfortable and secure lives. I'm glad to have a book with such positive encouragement."

—Dr. Philip Levin, Author of *Alternate Perspectives*

"I was amazed by the realistic solutions, and fascinated by the formula for Radical Negotiation that could help us resolve our nuclear issues on a global scale."

—Dr. Timothy Melton, Clinical Psychotherapist

"Wow, what a contribution! The scope is amazingly informative in many ways. I found it surprising that the book covers so much of what ails our planet."

—Dr. Michael Kuhar, Emory University Professor,
Author of *Research Ethics*

"Very thorough and really encompassing, Dr. Ryback investigates the phenomenon of global challenges from several perspectives, including a historical review of pandemics, climate change, social injustice, and conflict resolution. Written in a personal style to make the reading more interesting and enjoyable, he offers psychological insights into our awareness of how social media can affect what we believe. Each chapter is carefully written. Furthermore, what readers gain from reading the book is an overall impression that is a very rare, exquisite overview of the four challenges we now face. This book is for anyone who is interested in the phenomenon of surviving these challenges, and who isn't? It's worth thinking and talking about. The issue of disinformation resonates with our current political climate and overwhelms our popular culture. Every reader will take something personal from it. To borrow a metaphor from the book, disinformation and conflict resolution are now very jazzy topics."

—Dr. Renate Motschnig, University of Vienna Professor,
Author of *Effectiveness of Person-Centered Learning in the Age of the Internet*

"The topics that Ryback presents in this manuscript are of the utmost importance in today's world, and his book has promise to deliver effective strategies for his readers."

—Greenleaf Book Group

"Dr. David Ryback eloquently slices through the sludge that sickens our current reality, and offers clear, fresh, purposeful pathways for individuals, communities, and governments to rise out of the mire and transcend these personal and collective crises."

—Zoe Haugo, Film Director

"As Dr. Ryback reveals, the segments on disinformation in climate change, pandemics, justice, and nuclear threats are very relevant these days."

—Lieutenant Colonel Waldo Waldman, Author of the best-selling *Never Fly Solo*

"David Ryback has written a book covering the major issues of significance to both Americans and millions of people around the world. He analyzes the issues based on science but explained in easy-to-understand language with great sensitivity to each of the main issues. He presents possible solutions to these socio-political-economic-environmental conditions. There is more than enough information for critical debate leading to resolution for an optimistic future."

—David P. Leonard, CEO, Codacom Communications

"The little-known stories behind the scenes that shaped major world events make for a fantastic read. As an international technological entrepreneur, I could truly appreciate the history behind the big-picture events that Ryback reveals in this engaging book."

—Reginald Weiser, CEO, Positron Access Solutions Corporation

"This important book instills hope, confidence and a sense of new possibilities. It presents radical alternatives to our old ways of resolving conflicts and restoring global sanity."

—Dr. Susan Campbell, Author of *Beyond the Power Struggle*

"In this wonderful guide for tackling monumental problems, David Ryback reveals a broad and highly informed view. His "radical strategies" actually turn out to be quite thoughtful and intelligent. In the best sense, they are thorough, highly common-sense approaches to living in a world beset by challenges almost too overwhelming to believe. This is an important book for readers to follow. As a long-time activist, I found the book highly valuable as a resource. Each section could be a book by itself."

—Murray Dabby, Author of *Social Therapeutic Coaching*

"Very interesting book! And easy to read. I recommend it highly to anyone with a social conscience."

—Dr. Paul Schempp, University of Georgia, Author of *5 Steps to Expert*

"In *4 Global Crises*, David Ryback delves into the most critical issues facing society today. He combines relevant knowledge from his own experiences with those of other scholars to help readers answer some of today's pertinent questions. In his plan for Radical Negotiation to deter nuclear threat, he lays out both strategic and tactical steps for success. Readers can even apply these same skills to resolve troubling issues of conflict in their own lives."

—Ken Futch, Speaker Hall of Fame, Author of *Take Your Best Shot*

"Dr. Ryback once again sets the stage with his documented stories, stirring us toward greater awareness and possible changes for best results. His well-crafted positions for eliminating possibly disastrous outcomes are offered with sustainable measures for stopping the continued degradation of our planet. Spiritual reconnection and truth-telling are high on my list of why people should read this very timely book."

—Joe Sasso, Executive Coach

4 Global Crises: Radical Strategies for Dealing with Nuclear Threat, Racial Injustice, Pandemics, and Climate Change

by David Ryback, PhD

© Copyright 2023 David Ryback

ISBN 978-1-64663-952-6

All rights reserved. No part of this publication may be reproduced, stored in a retrieval system, or transmitted in any form or by any means—electronic, mechanical, photocopy, recording, or any other—except for brief quotations in printed reviews, without the prior written permission of the author.

Published by

3705 Shore Drive
Virginia Beach, VA 23455
800-435-4811
www.koehlerbooks.com

4 GLOBAL CRISES

Radical Strategies for Dealing with
Nuclear Threat, Unjust Killings, Pandemics,
and Climate Change

DAVID RYBACK, PHD
Author of *Putting Emotional Intelligence to Work*

VIRGINIA BEACH
CAPE CHARLES

TABLE OF CONTENTS

Introduction 1

Section I: Nuked 7

    Chapter One: Resolving Conflict: A Personal Account 9

    Chapter Two: Radical Negotiation: One Alternative
    to the Tragedy of Nuclear War 26

Section II: Murdered 41

    Chapter Three: Alternate Realities Collide Yet Help Explain
    the Black Lives Matter Movement 43

    Chapter Four: For and against the BLM Movement:
    A Coming Civil War? 58

    Radical Strategies: Our Response to Racial Injustice 74

Section III: Scorched 77

    Chapter Five: Scorched: Climate Change to Climate Crisis ... 79

    Chapter Six: The Atlantic Ocean is Running AMOC 92

    Chapter Seven: What, Me Worry? 104

    Radical Strategies: Our Response to Climate Change............ 114

Section IV: Vaxxed.. 121

    Chapter Eight: Trust in the Age of COVID 123

    Chapter Nine: The Challenge of COVID-19:
    Reinfection and Vaccines 134

    Chapter Ten: The Various Variants 143

    Radical Strategies: Our Response to Sheltering at Home
    due to COVID-19 Variants or Any Future Pandemic 154

    Overview and Update 159

Acknowledgments 173

References.. 174

To all my friends who kept me going when there were more questions than answers.

INTRODUCTION

When written in Chinese, the word crisis is composed of two characters—one represents danger, and the other represents opportunity.

—John F. Kennedy

"There are two problems for our species' survival," claimed social philosopher Noam Chomsky, "nuclear war and environmental catastrophe—and we're hurtling toward them." Then he uttered with grave concern, "Knowingly!"

There is a choice, and that makes us responsible. The author of this book doesn't feel very reassured by that statement. How do I—and you—navigate that terrifying path into the future? There must be a way to take charge and deal with such challenging issues that extends hope and some positive form of reassurance. I've given this much deep thought—loads of reflection and concern, plus many hours of research—and come up with strategies that have been shown to lead to positive outcomes. My approach is based on the science of psychology and is highly practical as well.

Now I offer this to you to consider as my gift, as both of us do our part to offer the resources I spell out here to those in our personal networks who influence and make up our political, social, scientific, or medical communities. Acting together, we can aspire to reduce the likelihood of nuclear conflict, remediate racial injustice, limit environmental damage, and mitigate medical disaster in the face of pandemics.

> My strategies are radical because they are highly unconventional and innovative in a deep (or radical) sense. They really work if applied diligently. And that is up to you.

Purpose

The purpose of this book is to offer you a way to shift from feeling fear and helplessness—a sense of urgency—to feelings of greater self-confidence—with a sense of opportunity—and, for those coping with social injustice, the acquisition of mutual support to bolster a protective sense of community.

Social media has created a tyranny of disinformation that alters and affects the way many of us see the world.

One productive way of dealing with the fear and uncertainty resulting from the four global crises is to take a closer look at what causes us to stress out on an ongoing basis. What if we could discover ways to overcome such stress by taking charge of the issues and transforming that sense of dread into one of mastery, competence, and self-confidence? That's what this book is all about.

Times change. On November 15, 2022, the United Nations celebrated the Day of Eight Billion. It took 300,000 years for the first billion people to populate our planet. That happened at the beginning of the nineteenth century, just when Beethoven performed his *Third Symphony* for the first time. By 1927, there were two billion souls on Earth, and four billion by 1974, a number that had doubled to eight billion by 2022. The UN projects that we will be approaching nine or ten billion about twenty-five years from now.

What are your greatest concerns about the state of our planet? As we began the year of 2023, it seemed that more than half of us were concerned about the pollution of rivers, lakes, and oceans. Three-quarters worried about global conflict between superpowers, especially nuclear war with Russia. And what about all those third-world nations that are affected by the high cost of food and possible mass starvation, in part because of Russia's invasion of Ukraine and its effects on the international food market and supply chain.

The welfare of our planet is not a casual consideration. It is, of course, more important than any other topic we can imagine. If nothing is done, there is grave danger lurking: Our planet Earth may cross the tipping point in terms of climate change. Many of us could be killed off by some pandemic or any of its variants as has happened in recorded medical history (see beginning of Chapter Nine for details). Our democracy, for which we've fought several fierce wars, can falter if we don't stand up for it. And Heaven forbid the outcome of nuclear war.

> We dare not be mere spectators in this horrific spectacle called *The End of Earth*.

These four ongoing major crises affect us all—up close and personal. In this book, we'll look at exactly how the conflict in politics leading to threats of nuclear war, racial prejudice, climate change, and pandemic variants all affect our daily lives.

In 1798, Thomas Malthus feared that any population growth on our fragile planet beyond 800 million people would result in widespread famine, but that prediction and several similar ones since then, like that of his defender David Ricardo in 1811, have fallen by the wayside, discarded as wrong. This occurred most likely because their estimates were based on the indices of their time and were uninformed considering what we now know.

Every morning, across the globe, we awaken to disinformation about the four crises that will not go away. Let's take a look at each one:

- **Nuclear threats** due to international misunderstandings, conflicts, or outright aggression, such as when Russia invaded

Ukraine on February 24, 2022. The fear of nuclear holocaust has become vivid once again. Threats from nations such as China, Russia, North Korea, Iran are becoming more prevalent.

- **Rampant injustice** that affects marginalized people everywhere. An increasing number of minority citizens fear leaving their homes lest they become the targets of believers in conspiracy theories that invite White supremacists to shoot them dead while casually shopping for food, as happened in Buffalo, New York in June of 2022. A sense of dread begins to pervade their lives.

- **Climate change** at which our planet sees temperatures so high that people in India and Pakistan fall dead in the streets because of heat stroke. The increase in frequency and intensity of forest fires, flooding, droughts, and extremes in high temperatures across the globe remind us that we may be beyond the tipping point, yet many in our government see the current climate crisis as a hoax. The threat is both the climate change itself as well as our government's lack of action to manage it. Most of our major cities have heat waves that last forty-five days longer than they did only fifty years ago. Extreme rainfall has increased by more than 50 percent over the past ten years. Arctic ice has declined by 95 percent since 1995. (See Chapter Six if you find this hard to believe.)

- **A pandemic** that continues to haunt us. We fear reinfection with each new variant of COVID-19, despite vaccinations, social isolation, and masking. Just as we breathe a sigh of relief about not having to wear masks, we discover that the latest variants are rearing their ugly heads with the onslaught of potentially high reinfection rates. Is there no end to this pandemic?

Across the planet, we will be forced to cope with these four global challenges for the foreseeable future. Despite their significance, we, as individuals acting alone, cannot heal the oceans, protect the wildlife—or even one another—nor can we prevent nuclear war. But what *can* we do?

Here's how this book can help you.

Benefits to You, the Reader

This book will offer you successful solutions to help resolve the crises, and you'll have the opportunity to transform the fears and stresses related to these challenges into a greater sense of confidence and mastery of your life moving forward.

In this book, you will learn to take charge by discovering:

- An approach to conflict resolution in the political arena that holds great promise for "One Alternative to Nuclear Planetary Suicide." This was the title of a popular paper that I coauthored with the eminently respected pioneer of effective communication, Dr. Carl Rogers.
- How minority groups can be more self-sustaining and self-confident so that they are much less likely to become victimized.
- Several recommendations to diminish the acceleration of climate change, even if some say that we're too close to the point of no return.
- How to deal more effectively, comfortably, and especially constructively with COVID-19, should we be faced with more variants, or even other yet-unknown pandemic-inducing viruses.

So, let's move directly to the crisis of nuclear threat and later to social injustice, climate change that envelops our planet, and finally to the threat of pandemics.

SECTION I:

NUKED

THREE PRINCIPLES OF RADICAL NEGOTIATION TO DETER NUCLEAR THREAT

CHAPTER ONE

Resolving Conflict: A Personal Account

Humanity is just one misunderstanding, one miscalculation away from nuclear annihilation.

—UN Secretary-General António Guterres

We will not learn how to live together in peace by killing each other's children.

—Jimmy Carter

The difficulties of peace are better than the agony of war.

—Menachem Begin

For the past several decades following the Cuban Missile Crisis in 1962, the fear of nuclear warfare seemed to go underground and atomic warhead rattling quieted down considerably. But, since Russia's invasion of Ukraine in February of 2022, the threat of nuclear warfare has reared its treacherous head.

At this point, Russia and the US combined own 91 percent of all nuclear weapons, but China is rushing to compete, planning on doubling its nuclear arsenal to 200 warheads by 2034. This leaves the other six, France, India, Pakistan, Israel, North Korea, and the UK, to make up the rest of the nuclear community. One remaining threat, a crucial one, is Iran, apparently nine-tenths of the way to achieving weapons-grade fuel.

How to Fail at Conflict Resolution

Let's begin with what does *not* work in the process of conflict resolution, whether in the private interaction between a couple, or any conflict in the business world and even at the international, political level where nuclear conflict is a possibility. If you want to know what most individuals do when faced with conflict, here are the five steps:

1. Blame the other party.
2. Let the anger take over.
3. Never listen to the other side.
4. Make your decisions arbitrary.
5. Repeat the cycle over and over.[1]

And the result is predictable, whether in your marriage, with your children, at work, or wherever. When international conflict takes place, this process can lead to the death of many, many innocent people.

We're all tired of seeing people kill one another—including children—on such large scales, whether it's Palestine, Afghanistan, Yemen, Ethiopia, Myanmar, or Iraq, not to mention Russia's invasion of Ukraine.

The Most Imminent Challenge of All

In this first section, we'll explore the application of Dr. Carl Rogers's three principles of trust in a personalized form, as I use them in my own consulting practice. When applied skillfully, these principles can transform communication, whether between two people or within groups. They can even save nations from committing homicide on an international basis by having the leaders meet with one another and learn to communicate on a more humane basis, as did Prime Minister Begin and President Sadat in achieving the Camp David Peace Accords between Egypt and Israel under the direction of President Jimmy Carter.[2] Every person, group, and even nation has its own rationale as a basis for its values, policies, and decisions.

> By creating a forum to hear these unique "realities," we can use this approach to allow for deeper communication, work out differences, and even save lives.

Underlying the theme of this section is the concept of *excellence in listening*, an extraordinary component of all effective communication, from one-on-one to international negotiations. It is an exchange of views and a process of interaction that can be applied to all circumstances, bringing opposites together through emotionally open "argument." I call this unique concept *Radical Negotiation*. Hopefully, this will excite your creative juices and help you view your life in a more stimulating, and jazzy, context. (This jazzy element will be explored later on.)

Radical Negotiation: A Revolution in International Conflict Resolution

To explore the deeper challenges of applying Rogers's principles of trust, it might be very helpful to look at the "devil's-in-the-details" aspects, meaning those that deviate from the expected and which create what might seem like insurmountable obstacles. How does one apply a theoretically simple approach to the real world of human complexity? Here's how President Jimmy Carter handled the nuts and bolts of "reality," as described in his book, *Keeping Faith*.

1) ***Protected candor:*** First, Carter did his best to create an ambience of camaraderie. He encouraged accepting one another's delegations as human beings as well as diplomats by organizing the meals in a way that forced some degree of friendly interaction. The delegations ate together in informal settings, allowing shared activities after the meals, such as chess and bike riding. In this way, trust could build more quickly than if they had been separated outside of the negotiation talks. The two sides could more easily develop empathy for their former enemies and allow for growing rapport, which could spill over into the negotiation process itself.

2) ***Theme of authentic emotion:*** Carter allowed for the full expression of strong emotion to enhance the natural flow of passion, like a full-throated Beethoven symphony. There were moments of intense frustration and the expression of anger without reservation.

    Here's how Carter accomplished this daunting task: He created a safe space by excluding the press so that Begin and Sadat could more easily vent their authentic emotions regarding their enemies. Begin and Sadat were invited to reveal their true feelings about the conflicting demands between the two nations. When intense emotions arose, Carter welcomed them and allowed their full expression. This way, each nation could get a better sense of the restraints that each leader was forced to deal with in terms of reporting back to their respective parliaments.

3) *Acceptance of disagreement:* Unlike a conventional negotiation process, there was allowance for the expression of differences that lay beneath the respective points of view, fully declared, even when this was quite uncomfortable. Carter was somehow able to bring a sense of resolution to the situation, sometimes with the use of humor. Here is a prime example:

    > At the very outset, President Sadat insisted on reading an eleven-page paper to the other two leaders. It was a

shocking document, to which the Israelis especially listened with some horror. It showed none of the conciliatory attitudes that had brought Sadat to Camp David. It presented a position that the Israelis could not possibly accept. Carter, too, was astonished at the belligerent and rigid stand that it took.

The silence was long and heavy. "I tried to break the tension by telling Begin that if he would sign the document as written, it would save all of us a lot of time," Carter later wrote. "I was surprised when everyone broke into gales of genuine laughter."[2]

4) ***Accepting defeat ... temporarily:*** As a matter of fact, there were times when one or the other delegations was fed up and ready to quit the process.

At one point, when the talk became extremely heated, "all restraint was now gone," Carter wrote. "Their faces were flushed, and the niceties of diplomatic language and protocol were stripped away ... Begin had touched a raw nerve, and I thought Sadat would explode. He pounded the table."

"The mood of anger gave way to sadness and disappointment," Moshe Dayan, Israeli Foreign Minister, later commented, as there was a realization that the conference might well fail.[2]

5) ***Connecting through trust:*** But Carter took on the role of a leader using the three principles of Radical Negotiation.

On the last day of the conference, when it seemed that all efforts were failing, and when Prime Minister Begin was adamant about not signing anything and decided to give up and leave Camp David without any resolution, Carter took a very personal step.

Carter was stymied. He did not want this challenge to end in costly failure. After much meditation on the matter,

Carter decided on a plan of action. He grabbed a folder on his desk.

Photographs had been taken of the three leaders together and Sadat had autographed all of them. Begin had requested that three be autographed for his grandchildren. Since Sadat had already signed them, Carter decided to personalize the inscriptions even further, signing each one of them.

He then went to Begin's cabin and found him sitting on the front porch, very distraught and nervous because the talks had finally broken down at the last minute.

He approached Begin and they began talking, their expressions forlorn about the impending failure of the talks. Then Carter pulled out the photos to show them to Begin.

"I handed him the photographs," Carter later wrote. "He took them and thanked me. Then he happened to look down and saw that his granddaughter's name was on the top one. He spoke it aloud and then looked at each photograph individually, repeating the name of the grandchild I had written on it. His lips trembled and tears welled up in his eyes. He told me a little about each child and especially about the one who seemed to be his favorite.

"We were both emotional as we talked quietly for a few minutes about grandchildren and about war."[2]

Carter asked Begin if he could imagine his granddaughters in the distant future telling their children about their grandfather being responsible for peace in the mid-East. Begin's attitude shifted immediately, and he decided to accept the language of the draft he had previously rejected. The road to success was now in progress.[2]

This was a turning point, and Prime Minister Begin shook hands with Carter, deciding to resume the process, even walking over to Sadat's cabin by himself to pick up the pieces, re-entering the friendlier disposition of the previous days.

This was the "authentic and yet highly regardful dialogic interactions" described by social scientists Renate Motschnig-Pitrik and Godfrey Barett-Lennard in their research on effective communication in which each party constructs a shared meaning based on the other party's statements in a reciprocal process. They refer to this as a "coactualizing process" in which both parties take responsibility for building the mutual understanding between them leading to resolution of conflict.[3]

Carter was a bit concerned. Would they end up with disagreements and fighting once again? He decided to intercede and walked over to Sadat's cabin to see how Begin had fared. "He was quite happy," wrote Carter, "as he told me that they had had a 'love feast' and that Sadat had agreed to Begin's language on the Knesset [Israeli parliament] vote."[2]

6) ***Personal engagement***: Carter's application of the three principles of Radical Negotiation, despite the long narrative of betrayal and hostile emotions.

These researchers on the deep complexities of effective communication, Motschnig-Pitrik and Barett-Lennard, differentiate the actualizing tendency for self, i.e., ego-based point of view, from the coactualizing dynamic in which parties connect with mutual perspectives. It is based on a growing trust in "a continually unfolding process in an interdependent relationship."

"A climate of trust tends to pervade such relationships . . . in a warmth of engagement both at the individual level and in the relationship itself and is likely to be gainfully perceived by others yet with peaks of strong presence and valleys where it is not apparent."[3] Building trust, in other words, takes effort, as President Carter revealed, and so does maintaining that level of trust over time.

During the negotiation process, Carter continually took notes on the ongoing interactions. Whenever a stalemate came up, or an emotional blowup that threatened to end the negotiations, he would read aloud his notes to give both sides a more objective view of what each side was trying to accomplish. Carter could read the nonverbal messages and integrate those into his notes without being obvious about it. Occasionally, he would read his notes out loud to the entire group. That way, each side could have a sense of the constraints binding the other side. This sensitive aspect that helped overcome otherwise daunting challenges has never been described in any literature on Carter's process. Yet this is an essential part of the process of building trust and overcoming antagonistic perspectives.

This indispensable aspect, or *sine qua non*, cannot be taken for granted if this process is to succeed in other negotiations between nations in conflict.

> The leader or facilitator has the responsibility of communicating the deeper feelings of both sides whatever format that takes, whether through reading notes aloud, talking privately with each side, or sharing with both sides simultaneously the observed subtleties of nonverbal messages in a way that ruffles no feathers.

Carter maintained a totally impartial stance, never taking any disposition of his own to interfere with the process. His total focus was on resolving the differences and not on some predetermined outcome that he might have preferred. His impartial stance was tested over time, and never did it fail. He was totally in service of allowing each side to state its position, emotional intensity notwithstanding. He was able to make both sides feel free to share their views as openly as they could.[2]

7) ***Something new***: In the end there was successful agreement between the delegations, resulting in the Camp David Peace Accords between the two formerly bitter enemies. Carter was able to muster enough trust between the two parties to transcend the tradition of enmity between the countries. His emotions of caring (about peace) and seeking (for a solution) overcame the fear and rage (after decades of war) between the two nations—all this achieved by fostering trust despite the negative emotions.

Note, from the above example, how this can be made to occur between enemies, as Carter proved. Photos in the public media, taken at the celebration of the success of the Peace Accords, reveal clearly the authentic caring President Sadat of Egypt and Prime Minister Begin of Israel had built between them and, with it, a growing sense of trust, despite decades of prior wars and bitter hostilities. Now we have a close view of how the trust developed over the thirteen days of negotiation.[4]

The peaks of strong presence and valleys were there, and Carter was able to overcome those challenges, even when, as Carter explained, "almost every discussion of any subject deteriorated into an unproductive argument, reopening old wounds of past political or military battles."[2]

As Richard Rovere later wrote in *The New Yorker*, official protocol can give way to top-down, emotionally open dialogue once the ritual of opening statements has been accomplished.[5]

The one undeniable component of Radical Negotiation is a strong leader to facilitate and support this intimate process through its inevitable ups and downs, including the prospect of facing failure at certain intense moments. Like Carter, such a leader must use all of her or his creative resources to appeal to the deeper conscience of the discouraged party, to reconsider and examine some crucial aspect of the bigger picture that justifies bending over backward to allow for challenging and seemingly impossible compromises to reach any agreement. Such leadership is the *sine qua non* of the entire process.

Toward the end of 2021, President Biden began to reach out to China to initiate talks that would prevent inadvertent nuclear conflict should there be any accidental mishaps in communication about weapon usage as China builds its arsenal.[6] Hopefully, trust will continue to grow in the areas rife with international conflict, of which there are so many. Rebuilding trust requires authenticity, dedication . . . and plenty of hard listening.

Israel and some Arab states are now trusting neighbors and even joining forces against the common enemy, Iran[7], which is coming closer and closer to becoming a nuclear antagonist and an existential threat to the West[8], unless we can use the Radical Negotiation skills that we are considering here.

A Personal Account of The Three Principles of Radical Negotiation

About a year ago, I was charged with attempting to break a deadlock between the CEO of an organization and one of his direct reports. The two had opposing values in terms of leadership style and the conflict had been ongoing for close to a year. Something had to give.

Victor, the CEO, was steadfast in his belief that he had all the right answers and that Pam, his direct report, was totally off the rails.

Pam, from her perspective, thought that Victor (not their real names) was so far from her version of reality, that she accused him (behind his back, of course) of being mentally imbalanced. The stakes were high, but I felt quite comfortable approaching this challenge.

Why? Although I had worked with similar issues before with an excellent record of resolving them, no matter how difficult, this time I planned to pay special attention to what I was doing so I could share the details of my experience with others. These were the skills I learned from Carl Rogers over the years, skills that you, too, can learn to practice the art of conflict resolution and the building of trust. The best way to deal with issues arising from a breakdown in trust is to do a deep dive into its roots and bridge the gap between the antagonistic parties.

By the end of this encounter, which took a few days, I could see Rogers's three basic principles emerge more clearly in my awareness. Though simple to describe and understand, they can create near miracles when they're aptly applied in an authentic yet courageous manner. I've practiced and learned this over time, and you can too, if you decide to do so.

One pattern became clear. Once the antagonists were able to make their points of view known, and shared their own perspectives, including their vulnerable issues, with authentic emotion, then those around the table seemed to focus in on what solutions might be forthcoming. Their body positions changed, as they leaned in a bit more.

Over time, a keen observer who was watching me carefully would realize three things. First off, I'm more likely to share my awareness of some dynamics of subtle but definite and pervasive conflict among some individuals in the room. Even though it goes unmentioned, this might be uncomfortable to the others until I finally do bring it to their attention and enlighten them. And, when I do, there's something like a sigh of relief that some tension has been resolved. If there's an "elephant in the room," I bring it to light. It's crucial to have the courage for this and not wait for the "right" moment. It might have to do with some subtle feeling that is somewhat uncomfortable for the participants, yet important to the topic at hand. This awareness as a skill can be learned, and the courage to bring it to light can be acquired through proper mentoring.

The second item is a persistent focus on the topic of emerging importance rather than being derailed by any side issues. When tension rises because of some uncomfortable issue, it's normal for someone in the group to go off on a side tangent to relieve the tension. But it's always important to return to the relevant matter, despite any group discomfort with the issue. This keeps the relevant issue in focus, no matter how uncomfortable it might be. I do this in a confident manner, just sharing my true, inner feeling in the moment about whatever this issue happens to be. I focus on what appears on the grid of my emotional awareness of the relevant topic.

The third item of importance is to demonstrate a keen awareness of anyone in the group whose body language or facial expression reveals some feeling but who isn't expressing it, perhaps because of shyness or feeling some form of social reservation.

I typically draw out such individuals by inviting them to speak up. I might say, "John, I notice that you may have some feelings about this topic. I, for one, would be quite interested in your thoughts. Would you feel comfortable sharing them?" I gently bring these people out, encouraging them to speak up on their own though they might not otherwise do so. The ambience of the overall group interaction subsequently becomes more flowing and receptive to others sharing more personal points of view.

To accomplish the above, I must transcend my own ideas, opinions and desires while being of service to others, and to focus my awareness on others' ideas, opinions, and desires. That's not easy for most of us to accomplish, and it took me years to acquire this attribute.

This combination of skills, for lack of a better term, marks the path to allowing others to dig into their own power toward greater personal trustworthiness. If you can model trust just by being yourself with your natural, indisputable honesty, then you can do it as well, just as Rogers did.

Most people need time, sometimes years, to reach and develop a stage of total, inner honesty about their feelings in the moment. In forming relationships, we are like onions, slowly peeling off one protective layer at a time, over many meetings with someone with whom we want to develop a deeper relationship. But it is possible to allow yourself to be at an advanced level of emotional openness as a way of being from the start.

Creating a Safe Space for Radical Negotiation

Simply put, I began to realize that if you choose to adopt this style of communication, you can create a safe space for others to take the risk of growing their authentic selves with greater integrity and whatever other powers come along with that, just as Rogers did.

This disciplined style of building connection, even to conquer conspiracies of lies, I'm convinced, can work in most situations if both parties are open to being honest in the interaction. We can learn from Rogers and promulgate it to those who can learn from us when we're in positions of leadership.

We can all learn to do this by proclaiming to ourselves, as we head into a meeting:

1. I will share my authentic feelings with others and demonstrate a caring attitude toward the people and issues to which I choose to give my attention.
2. I will focus clearly on what is relevant and important at the time, and not let trivial distractions pull the group away from what really matters in the moment of engagement. The choice to stay with what is relevant helps to resolve issues rather than allow them to drag on.
3. I will make it a priority to hear all voices, especially the quiet, reserved ones, so that the occasional attention seekers do not monopolize the time and focus of a meeting.

> All this takes courage as well as sensitivity and awareness, along with a selflessness that looks to support the viewpoints of others rather than defend one's own when conflicts, large or small, arise.

Clearly, these skills are unique and rarely come naturally to anyone, though they seem to have been quite natural for Rogers. Yet they can be learned if you decide to practice them on an ongoing basis, as they become more familiar and reliable over time.

One more thing. Expect nothing in return for your emotional generosity, not even others' attention. This might be argued to be a fourth component of this skillful approach.

This caring enterprise creates a safe place for the truth of any matter under dispute to shine through. This rare combination of human qualities can result in highly productive and valuable outcomes, despite how simply put are the skills in bringing it about.

Applying the Three Principles of Radical Negotiation

The outcome, when this approach is sustainable, is the resolution of conflict which then allows for people to grow together in mutually satisfying progress.

At this point, allow me to share my three principles of Radical Negotiation, as I call them, so we can see the process more clearly.

> **FIRST PRINCIPLE OF RADICAL NEGOTIATION:**
> Acknowledging the other's point of view → Empathy → Trust

The first principle involves understanding and appreciating the other's point of view, a relatively simple approach to what we characterize as *active listening*—almost common sense.

> **SECOND PRINCIPLE OF RADICAL NEGOTIATION:**
> Exploration of what others express → Resolution of conflict

The second principle involves something that takes a bit more energy in engagement—going deeper to feel what the other is experiencing at a nonverbal level about the conflict at hand, including her or his values and inner needs that are not normally expressed to others. This sensitivity to subtle cues must be done with extreme awareness of the individual's readiness to receive such information. By sharing what you sense about these needs, the other feels recognized at a deeper, personal level so that accepting these "newly discovered" traits reveals a greater sense of self-acceptance and inner confidence to resolve differences. This allows for less defensive positions about the conflict.

These traits can be, in a sense, the individual's personal, inner feelings that are most likely accurate but not noticed by the others. They are part of the person, but not shared in any obvious way with the rest of the world.

Now, here's the third, the components of which were described earlier:

> **THIRD PRINCIPLE OF RADICAL NEGOTIAION:**
> Opening ideas and feelings in a safe space → Growing trust and the greater likelihood of resolution of conflict

The third principle is the most powerful. It involves a combination of skills:

- Your ability to focus sharply on your best perspective of the dynamic of the group and its progress regarding the topic at hand, a growing feeling in you that persists for a while, rather than an impulsive emotion. As you begin practicing this, pay attention to any feeling in you (about the issue at hand) that continues for a while. That can validate your feeling, before you share it with the group. You won't always have this awareness, and that's okay. But, when you do, it's worthwhile sharing it. It'll most likely to happen when you sense something going on that is important to the topic, yet no one else is mentioning it.

- The courage to share your deep awareness of what is important and relevant to the group in the moment and fighting off distractions that others might bring to the table to assuage their own discomfort about the tension at hand.
- The selflessness and confidence to invite other "quiet" voices that might not ordinarily speak up against the very confident members who might otherwise "outshine" them. This is a simple, yet courageous and thoughtful skill that you can easily develop by merely focusing on the potential value of these soft voices and picturing yourself a kind of guardian. This will further garner respect from the group members that your focus is not ego-driven but rather for the benefit of all.

This tripartite approach can result in a very powerful leadership style. The first and second principles may only involve one-on-one interactions. The third involves a group dynamic and requires a great deal of self-confidence, built over times of trial and error, more natural for some (like Rogers) than others. Only personal experience will reveal where you find yourself on this continuum.

> The theme that runs through all this is the ability to avoid judging others' values, but rather to understand their perspective through their eyes.

Of course, these same skills can be used in dealing with opposing views on many matters, including the topics of other sections in this book, such as resolving conspiracies of trust relating to social injustice, opinions about vaccines, whether climate change is a hoax, etc.

With Putin's issues with Ukraine, North Korea brandishing its intercontinental missiles, and Iran threatening to gain the capacity for atomic warfare, this opportunity to resolve the crisis of trust could hardly be more topical. A return to trust between the US and its antagonists—the Peoples Republic of China, Iran, and Russia—might also benefit by these same principles of Radical Negotiation, not to mention the ongoing skirmishes around the globe that could use the replacing of bullets with words of compassion.

In this chapter, we introduced the concept of Radical Negotiation within the context of nuclear conflict. We started with what not to do (but what typically does occur) and quickly followed with what to do, namely the three principles of trust necessary for effective conflict resolution. We used the example of the success of the Camp David Peace Accords organized by President Jimmy Carter. Then we shared in precise detail how the three principles can be applied in the context of international conflict leading to nuclear threat.

In the next chapter, we'll review these basic concepts and put the meat of theory on the bones of what we've laid out so far. We'll go deep into what's been learned in the decades since Rogers's early writings that makes the application so challenging. Then we'll bring the focus closer to the present to speculate on how Putin might respond to Radical Negotiation.

CHAPTER TWO

Radical Negotiation: One Alternative to the Tragedy of Nuclear War

It's a near miracle that nuclear war has so far been avoided.

—Noam Chomsky

If you want peace, don't talk to your friends. Talk to your enemies.

—Desmond Tutu

Let's do a deeper dive into the concept of Radical Negotiation. We'll look more closely at the details and their theoretical ramifications for application in the real world of international conflict, continuing our use of the Camp David Peace Accords as the primary example of the success of the approach.

In the *Harvard Business Review*, Carl Rogers wrote: "We can achieve real communication and avoid this evaluative tendency when we listen with understanding. This means seeing the expressed idea and attitude from the other person's point of view, sensing how it feels to the person, achieving his or her frame of reference about the subject being discussed."[1] Rogers doesn't mention the term "ego," as in the need to ignore one's ego, but that's an important concept, one which creates great challenge for most of us.

Let's review what we've just learned in this past chapter. How would we apply Rogers's active listening process, so simplistic in its theoretical approach, to the hard test of reality? By reviewing this material in detail and putting it in the context of research on effective communication, we can better lock in the application of this important information on Radical Negotiation. Although this involves some repetition, it is worthwhile since the application of this model is so important for understanding the details of the Camp David Summit.

What if the two nations that had experienced conflict with one another for hundreds of years truly hated one another and this hatred was intensified over the years by sneak attacks on both sides—the Six-Day War of 1967 initiated by the Israelis and the Yom Kippur War of 1973 initiated by the Egyptians? They spoke different languages, yet they both claimed the same land as their own with deep religious and historical roots.

As we discussed in the last chapter, that is what President Jimmy Carter took on when he attempted peace talks between Israel and Egypt, using the exact principles that Rogers advocated—listening with open hearts as each side revealed its most intense emotional reactions to the other.[2]

Carter's plan was to bring these hostile nations together in an informal setting and steer the antagonism between the two parties toward conciliation by building a sense of trust between them.[3]

This approach would involve an invitation by a third party, President Carter, to start the process. There would need to be a revolutionary approach, akin to Rogers's style of open and forthright communication, with a goal of conflict resolution. Both parties would need to embrace this theme. Just as in any Rogerian process, there would be the aim of allowing for a growing trust level to proceed toward a mutually acceptable compromise between two very different perspectives—acceptable not only to the participants but also to their respective nations' parliaments. Finally, the revolutionary and radical approach would need to withstand the intense emotions of bitter anger and suspicion based on the fractured history between the two nations.

a) *Invitation*: Carter invited both delegations to his Camp David site, a neutral retreat-type setting that allowed for shared meals, casual contact during walks, bike riding, and evening participation in such games as chess. A highly informal environment without protocol or assigned seats at meals would lead to a growing sense of trust, Carter hoped. To enhance this growing trust, Carter decided not to invite the press, so candor might be more forthcoming.

b) *Cohesive theme*: Though there was no set agenda, the theme of the meeting was profoundly well understood. To foster a return to trust, a rigid format was considered unnecessary, and issues would be considered as they naturally arose, allowing a more free-flowing process.

> Expression of strong emotion through the process of Radical Negotiation is encouraged to enhance the natural flow of passion.

c) *Movement to agreement*: In this challenging dialogue, there were moments of laughter and warm acceptance but there were also moments of tension and intense frustration and anger. Just as in jazz, there were moments when the "notes" didn't always connect. As a matter of fact, there were times when one or the other delegations was fed up and ready to quit the process. But Carter took on the role of a Rogerian and put them back on track. President Carter was a lover of popular music and enjoyed inviting musicians to perform at the White House more than any prior president. He saw music as a wonderful medium for communication and used it as a metaphor for connection. He was able to navigate some terrible moments to successful turning points, just as jazz musicians find their *common theme* after experimenting with their individual contributions and improvisations.

d) *Something new*: In the end there was successful agreement between the delegations, resulting in the Camp David Peace Accords between the two formerly bitter enemies. Carter was able to muster enough trust between the two parties to transcend the tradition of enmity between the countries. His emotions of caring about peace and seeking a solution overcame the fear and rage, after decades of war between the two nations, all this achieved by fostering a return to trust despite the negative emotions.

A Jazzy Togetherness

Sometimes, listening to such "music" intuitively with the "third ear" can help decide whom to trust and whom not to trust.[4] Often it is not just what is being said, but, probably more important for building trust, how it is said and to what extent there is that "jazzy" togetherness, referred to as "constructive-constructivist conversation" by Dr. Nino Tomaschek of the University of Vienna, or "coactualization" as some psychologists refer to it.[5] A coactualizing process, according to these authors, provides for "a set of constructive relationships among a group of colleagues,"[6] making possible "authentic and yet highly regardful dialogic interactions" with "a self-organizing quality."[7]

What this means in lay terms is that two parties can both contribute to, or construct, a solution (constructive-constructivist conversation) as both take partial responsibility for its outcome (coactualization). "Highly regardful dialogic interaction" refers to respectful talk between the parties, despite the drama of negative feelings, in the process of growing trust. "Self-organizing quality" refers to the fact that both parties achieve their mutual agreement primarily of their own accord and not solely due to some outside force.

To fall back on the jazz metaphor, the two parties are grooving together, and each delegation listens to the music played by the other as they blend their music over time—coactualization—playing to the same beat and the same chords—highly regardful dialogic interaction—resulting in a unified melody that both have created simultaneously without outside help—a self-organizing quality.

Track II Diplomacy: About Grandchildren and About War

Note, from the above example, how this can also be made to occur between enemies, as Carter proved. Photos in the public media, taken at the celebration of the success of the Peace Accords, clearly reveal the genuine respect that President Sadat of Egypt and Prime Minister Begin of Israel had built between them and, with it, a growing return to trust, despite decades of prior wars and bitter hostilities. Let's take a close look at how the trust developed over the thirteen days of negotiation.

Exactly how did President Carter facilitate the coactualization process to build a bridge between the two bitter enemies and overcome a tragedy of mistrust? First off, Carter did not take this endeavor lightly. He risked his reputation as well as the prestige of his office in this "experiment" of what some referred to as Track II diplomacy. He was as much at risk as were the two antagonists he had invited to the process. Like Carl Rogers, he allowed himself to be vulnerable. And, like Carl Rogers, Jimmy Carter understood the power of empathy. "He's very good," said former US secretary of state, Madeleine Albright, "at putting himself in other people's shoes." And, she added, "He has a level of trust that you don't see in others."

Second, he was totally committed to the welfare of the two parties and demonstrated this when he took the time and effort to understand when either Begin or Sadat had reached their limit of compromise and were ready to abandon the negotiations. When Begin had declared he had decided to quit, Carter was determined to engage him with empathy and support. Begin and his entourage had their bags packed and were awaiting the shuttle to take them to the airport. Carter was stymied. What to do?

The scene so touching and significant that it merits repetition from the previous chapter. After much meditation in his office on the matter, Carter decided on a plan of action. He grabbed some photos of himself and personally inscribed them to each of Begin's grandchildren and walked over to his cabin. He approached Begin and they began talking about family, children and, of course, grandchildren. Then Carter pulled the photographs out of his folder to show them to Begin, at which point, "His lips began to tremble, and tears welled up in his eyes," Carter later wrote. "We were both emotional as we talked quietly for a few minutes about grandchildren and about war."[8]

The "Love Feast": A Warmth of Engagement

This was a turning point, and Begin shook hands with Carter, having decide to resume the process, even walking over to Sadat's cabin by himself to pick up the pieces. In doing so, he re-entered the "authentic and yet highly regardful dialogic interactions" described by Motschnig-Pitrik and Barett-Lennard above. Carter was a bit concerned. Would they end up with disagreements and fighting once again? He decided to intercede and walked over to Sadat's cabin to see how Begin had fared. "He was quite happy," wrote Carter, "as he told me that they had had a 'love feast' and that Sadat had agreed to Begin's language on the Knesset [Israeli parliament] vote."[8]

Building trust usually takes significant effort and time, thirteen full days of intense back-and-forth struggle between longtime enemies in this case.[9] The dynamics of this process of Radical Negotiation have been studied closely and examined carefully in an academic setting. The trusting relationship, whether between Prime Minister Begin and President Sadat or the two scientists doing research on this very issue of trust in their own experience, Renate Motschnig-Pitrik and G. Barrett-Lennard, was built despite "different experiences, styles, mother tongues, personal/family histories, and professional education and contexts."[10]

These authors differentiate the actualizing tendency for self—national pride and glory for each country, in this case—from the coactualizing dynamic in which individuals connect—the connecting to form the Peace Accords. It is based on a growing trust, in "a continually unfolding process in interdependent relationship. A climate of trust tends to pervade such relationships . . . in a warmth of engagement both at the individual level [when apart] and in the relationship itself [when interacting] and is likely to be gainfully perceived by others yet with peaks of strong presence and valleys where it is not apparent."[10] Building trust with Radical Negotiation, in other words, takes effort, as both Carl Rogers and President Carter revealed, and so does maintaining that level of trust over time.

Reopening Old Wounds: Violating All the Rules

Just like the two social scientists, Begin and Sadat certainly had different cultures, mother tongues, and political histories. In many ways, they were as different as one can imagine—Begin, an extraverted thinker and Sadat, an introverted feeling type—despite being geographical neighbors. Their "actualizing tendencies for self," or egos, were quite opposed to one another, each claiming the land of the other and having well-founded histories that justified their claims.[10] Yet the unfolding process, painful as it was, that Carter oversaw allowed for the eventual warm climate of trust that resulted in the interdependent relationship that led to the Peace Accords. The peaks of strong presence and valleys, described by the scientists, were there, and Carter was able to overcome those challenges, even when, as Carter explained, "almost every discussion of any subject deteriorated into an unproductive argument, reopening old wounds of past political or military battles."[8]

Sometimes the two antagonists refused to meet in the same room. Yet the "climate of trust," as described above, was achieved when Carter's leadership allowed for the expression of authentic emotion even though, as Carter wrote, "There was no compatibility between the two men."[8]

> **Trust demands authentic emotion, first and foremost,**

according to Rogers, and this was encouraged, even though the sworn enemies were engaging at the highest levels of international negotiation.

As Richard Rovere wrote in *The New Yorker*, "Carter's plans for Camp David violated all the rules of modern summitry."[11] Yet, if trust is to be achieved at this challenging level, then the rules must change, whether between warring nations, competing organizations, or members of a family.

More currently, Israel made peace with two more Arab nations—the United Arab Emirates and Bahrain,[12] marking "the dawn of a new Middle East," according to the former president of the United States.[13] Hopefully, trust will continue to grow in this area previously rife with international conflict. Trust requires authenticity . . . and plenty of hard listening.

Listening to the Music of Trust

As a colleague put it to me years ago, listening carefully "to understand the nuances" of the other[14] can help decide whom to trust and whom not to trust.

Jazz is a great metaphor for understanding Jimmy Carter's style of empathy. He loved music, but he had his priorities. When Willie Nelson came to perform at the White House, Carter could not attend personally because he was at Camp David creating the music that supported Begin and Sadat to come to terms with the Peace Accords. But Rosalynn was there and explained the reason for Jimmy's absence to the audience.[15]

Note, from the above vignette, how this nuanced listening can be made to occur between international enemies, as Carter proved, but also between those choosing to form any relationship of trust, whether in the boardroom or the bedroom. As the great jazz trumpetist Wynton Marsalis puts it, using jazz as a metaphor, "Ours is the art of listening and co-creating."[16] How true, and how relevant to Radical Negotiations, whatever the time or setting!

The Greatest Barrier: A Natural Tendency to Avoid Listening

In the *Harvard Business Review* article mentioned above, Harvard professor John Gabarro adds a postscript. He maintains that, though Rogers's message was a simple one, it wasn't an easy one to follow. One "reason . . . could be that this lesson is not so simple after all, that what the authors told us forty years ago is more difficult to do than it appears . . . *The greatest barrier to effective communication is the tendency to evaluate what another person is saying and therefore to misunderstand or to not really 'hear.'*"

In other words, even though we listen hard and hear the words, most of us still have feelings or emotions about ideas that are not ours and it is precisely those feelings are what get in the way of better communication. This is what some communication experts call noise.

> I believe the trick is in giving up our ego when we truly listen, at least temporarily, and there's the rub.

Rogers did this naturally, but it just is not easy for most others, sometimes me included.

We identify with our values and that makes it nigh impossible for most of us to hear others deeply as Rogers did. Gabarro goes on to say: "Checking the natural tendency to judge yields a better understanding of the person with whom you are communicating."[17] The natural tendency is to judge, he writes. It is quite definitely so in my own experience. That is the barrier to overcome, the overarching challenge that nations in conflict—the US with China, Russia, North Korea, Iran—need to battle, but with words and passion and emotion, not with firearms or bombs.

Where does trust fit in? As a rule, a minimum baseline of confidence in a third party, the individual in charge of the negotiation process, is needed to evoke the kind of trust that honest communication requires. This is especially true where there is a power imbalance, which tends to foster greater initial distrust.

What was learned over forty years? In Gabarro's opinion, "They must recognize that to make judgments, you must suspend judgment."[17] So, Rogers would insist, what he's talking about is not just listening carefully and sensitively, but also resonating to the other's feelings and values as if we were in that person's brain and heart, Rogers would insist, as if we're experiencing them as our own. For most of us, suspending judgment requires a judgment or decision to do so. We all need to make decisions about our behaviors and ultimate choices. These *are* judgments. So, the natural process is to negotiate the transactions between our values and those of the other.

Therein lies the great challenge.

Imagine, if you will, an attempt at using this "technology" to resolve the differences between President Vladmir Putin and his Western proponent, let's say President Biden or Jens Stoltenberg, the secretary-general of NATO. Could you imagine Putin actually feeling "heard" about his paranoid feelings of being overwhelmed by NATO-based democracies? Of course, the term *paranoid* would not be part of that interaction, but rather a highly unusual and exceptional openness to what's going on in Putin's heart and mind. The western proponent would be acting like a horse whisperer, not trying to claim dominance by force, but rather just following with trust-building distance, until the horse (or Putin) accepts the other as a friend rather than predator.

Of course, once the invasion of Ukraine began in earnest, there was no possibility of inviting Putin to negotiations.[18] Even French President Emmanuel Macron's requesting Chinese head Xi Jinping to act as an intermediary didn't work. According to the *Financial Times*, Putin had lost interest in diplomatic efforts to end the war, "infuriated after Ukraine sank the Moskva, the flagship of Russia's Black Sea Fleet."[19]

Putin would never submit to a therapist's couch, I think, but this might be the only way to get through to him and allow him an "escape ramp" from his addiction to power. Of course, all this would occur in absolute privacy from the press, etc., until a final resolution at which a meeting of minds might take place.

My best guess is that it might involve, in part, distancing NATO from Russia's borders with some kind of other arrangement, but with the infamous "trust but verify" agreement between Russia and the US.

> Like a renegade stallion, Putin may have no friends whom he could trust completely, so this "horse-whispering" approach might just be the right resolution for such an otherwise destructive mindset.

I'm sure this sounds very much like pie-in-the-sky hypothesizing. But it does make for some delicious food for thought.

No Shared Judgments: Demagoguery Instead of Listening

When we look at what happened at the election of President Trump in 2016, we see the opposite of cross-party communication and cooperation.

Trump arrived as a populist demagogue when there was a strong need for such an individual among those who considered themselves disenfranchised among the White population, spurred on mightily by QAnon. Since the ruling on Brown vs. the Board of Education, that group has metastasized over the years. White grievance found support as Trump made it more socially acceptable. And then many in the Republican Party followed his lead. What started as a party of small government, fiscal responsibility, self-reliance, a belief in a common good through unregulated capitalism, and a belief in the success of a White, male dominated society has morphed into what we see now—totally different. Now they appear to disdain democratic process. They see the need to hold on to power as priority.

Many in the mainstream press saw this as toxic, and so Trump characterized their reporting as fake news.

> Democracy allows for all voices, and Trump found his place within it, even with his preposterous claims.

The press could not ignore Trump's mesmerizing presence, as each week or day gave birth to more and more outlandish decisions on his part, staggering the imagination, and engaging readers and viewers, bringing more coin to the coffers of the media, particularly Fox News, which, as it turns out, were broadcasting what they believed their audience wanted rather than the blunt truth of it all.

In the last year of Trump's administration, the crises of COVID-19 and the killing of George Floyd fanned the flames of his flamboyant demagoguery. Trump's decision to avoid sharing the truth of COVID-19 because he didn't want to panic the population (or so he told Bob Woodward) contributed to many deaths, 400,000 Americans by the end of his administration. Pundits attempted to understand his modus operandi but could come to no conclusion that made any sense, except for a strong case of narcissism. This characterization was fortified by his niece's book on his family life, in which she describes him as "a petty, pathetic little man—ignorant, incapable, out of his depth, and lost in his own delusional spin."[20]

And so, we continue, with social media creating an echo chamber for political division that finds no end in the foreseeable future, about three-quarters of all Republicans believing that Trump's "landslide" victory was stolen in 2020. Meanwhile, White supremacists come out with playbooks on social media on how to recruit and radicalize more to their so-called tribe, including the possibilities of assassination of those they consider the enemy.

This is not limited to building Trump's political ego. Even a couple of years after the insurrection,[21] the influence of several paramilitary groups, including the 1st Amendment Praetorium, the Oath Keepers, and the Proud Boys, remains.[22] The influence of social media goes beyond that to include disinformation affecting our attitudes toward climate change, minority rights, and politics, since many of us get our information on those issues primarily through such media, along with mainstream networks.[23]

During the early weeks of the invasion of Ukraine by Russia, disinformation played a significant role, influencing attitudes toward one side or the other,[24] and fostering judgments for or against either side. Listening for "truth" is made even more complex in such a context.

As you might suspect, not all attempts at conflict resolution end up with success, even those modeled after President Carter's highly laudable achievement. In 2000, President Bill Clinton attempted another Camp David arrangement, following the protocol of Jimmy Carter's successful venture. He met with the Palestinian leader Yasir Arafat and Israeli Prime Minister Ehud Barak to come to a peace agreement between the two contingents. After two weeks of marathon negotiations between the two sides and their officers, which involved dealing with several difficult issues that, up to that point, were "really unprecedented . . . had long been considered off limits," according to President Clinton, the talks failed. "However, while we did not get an agreement," he concluded, "significant progress was made on the core issues."[25]

The remaining sticking point, after success on all the other issues, was the status of control over the historical Old City of Jerusalem, and on this point, Arafat could not compromise. If not for that one single item, the talks would have been successful, according to many of the participants. Before departing for his flight back to Israel, Arafat's aide, Saeb Erekat, admitted, "The prospect for agreement on all permanent-status issues are stronger than at any time in almost nine years."[25]

In this first section, I've shared with you my view of Carl Rogers's influence on conflict resolution, and we explored thoroughly how the expression of deep emotions, even the angry ones, helps explain the basics of conflict resolution through a return to trust.

Then we looked at the steps needed to create trust, applying those insights to one of the most challenging scenarios—reaching a peace accord between two warring and hostile nations—Israel and Egypt. Finally, we looked at how challenging it is to suspend judgment, which takes a judgment in and of itself, as was the case when President Jimmy Carter applied that to the success of the Camp David Peace Accords.

What I hope you take away with you is the importance of listening to someone's deeper feelings, not only to gain their trust by putting your ego aside but also to let the other take center stage, at least temporarily. This is what it takes to return to trust.

Here's a final takeaway: Next time you find yourself with your own personal version of a Begin-Sadat challenge, imagine what Carter or Rogers might do, and practice the skills offered in this section. You might just dodge a bullet—and replace it with trust to resolve any long-held or challenging dispute.

SECTION II:

MURDERED

SURVIVING RACIAL INJUSTICE

CHAPTER THREE

How Alternate Realities Collide Yet Help Explain the Black Lives Matter Movement

Shall we stop this bleeding?

—Abraham Lincoln, 1865, just prior to end of the Civil War

Every kind of peaceful cooperation among men is primarily based on mutual trust and only secondarily on institutions such as courts of justice and police.

—Albert Einstein

Racism is unfortunately still with us—we've got the footage.

—Bill Maher

Enough is enough!

—Keisha Lance Bottoms, mayor of Atlanta, following thirty-one shooting victims over a July 4th weekend

The pleas of an off-duty firefighter and emergency medical technician Genevieve Hansen rang hollow in the tense air in downtown Minneapolis, Minnesota on May 25, 2020. She merely wanted to be allowed to provide medical assistance to forty-six-year-old George Floyd as he was losing consciousness. She was completely ignored as police officer Derek Chauvin dug his knee even deeper into Floyd's neck, his left arm adding body weight to his kneeling leg.

She and another observer, Donald Williams II, phoned 911 to call the police *on* these police, as they witnessed the unbelievable killing.

> "Frustrated! Angry! Scared!" That's how the protesters felt on the night of May 28, 2020.

They had lost all trust in their local government in this Age of Misinformation, and particularly in the system of justice, following years of incidents which, if not for proof of the video would have gone unnoticed by the public. There was no tyranny of trust here—just the obvious treachery of another police officer taking liberty with his contempt for people of color under the guise of police duty.

Only three days earlier, Chauvin and two other officers had pinned down George Floyd while Officer Chauvin dug his knee into Floyd's neck for nine-and-a-half minutes. What was Chauvin's justification for the use of deadly force? According to him, Floyd had resisted getting into the patrol car. But this was because of his claustrophobia, his fear of being confined to small spaces. His last utterances before dying were "Please" and "Mama."

A year and a half later, just before Thanksgiving Day, 2021, there was another court case involving a video of Whites killing a Black victim. This was the trial against three Georgia men who had followed a Black twenty-five-year-old Ahmaud Arbery as he jogged through their White neighborhood in a small community in Glyn County in February of 2020 and then cornered and shot him at close range as Arbery tried to defend himself against the so-called citizen's arrest. The outcome of this trial was something to be thankful for when, a day later, we celebrated Thanksgiving. The three attackers were found guilty of their crimes after ten days of testimony and sentenced up to life in prison, thanks in part to the finely tuned argument of prosecutor, Linda Dunikoski, as she addressed the conservative values of the local jury.

Except for the videos in both incidents, most likely no case for justice could have been made. In the first case, this obscene act of one individual officer's contorted mind might have fallen under the radar of disturbing police acts that so many others have. No, no conspiracy of trust here, except for defense attorney Eric Nelson trying to find a morsel of evidence to justify what his client had done in full view of witnesses to the fact. So certain was officer Derek Chauvin that he would get away with his disproportionate response to holding someone of color under arrest, that the presence of the cameras didn't affect his actions a bit.

At the trial beginning March 22, 2021, Officer Chauvin's defense attorney Eric Nelson left no stone unturned in his effort to find some way of creating a rationale for his client as he riddled witnesses with questions aimed to belittle their experience of watching Mr. Floyd die as he was choked to death in the infamous video scene. Of course, at the end of the day, Chauvin was found guilty, along with the three officers—Tou Thao, J. Alexander Kueng, and Thomas Lane—who were there as well, two actually aiding Chauvin in his restraint of Floyd and the other keeping bystanders back and failing to intervene.

Chauvin was later tried on a civil basis in the summer of 2022 and sentenced to twenty-one years in jail to be served concurrently with his criminal conviction of April 2021 for twenty-two-and-a-half years of jail time.

> What makes this age of reporting different from last generation's era is the ubiquity of surveillance opportunities, primarily by personal cell phones as well as the body cameras worn by more and more police officers.

Controversies between police and citizens can now be more accurately seen and reported. The iconic video of the knee-on-the-neck incident was taken by a young bystander, Darnella Frazier, not a reporter and not a police officer. Police videos did not initially appear in the court scene of George Floyd's death. Darnella's efforts later won her a Special Citation by the Pulitzer Prize committee.

The Video That Shook the World

Just three days prior to the beginning of the protests, the iconic video of forty-four-year-old police officer Derek Chauvin pressing his knee into the neck of forty-six-year-old George Floyd, resulting in his death, went viral adding to the death of the element of trust that had been brewing for years.

The words the video recorded as he lay on the street, included "I can't breathe, man. Please!" and, most profoundly impressing those who cared, was the word, "Mama," that Floyd uttered in ultimate despair. A final look at the video revealed that the phrase, "I can't breathe," was repeated over twenty times.

As it turned out, the police officers determined that Floyd had no pulse after about six minutes of being knelt upon, and the knee was not moved away for another three minutes and twenty-nine seconds.

A Historical Precedent

Let's take a shift in focus for a moment. Imagine you're joining me in a time machine, taking us back about seventy-seven years or so. Here we go.

World War II was in full force. American soldiers were brought to the European front to do battle with the Nazis, risking their own lives in the process. Over 400,000 of these brave men never made it home. Among the fighting forces were Black Americans, and among those was one young, somewhat shy and reserved, always polite soldier known to his friends in uniform as Isaac. He went to fight at the age of nineteen. Now he was twenty-three.

As American soldiers returned from serving their nation

overseas during World War II, they returned to a country they hardly recognized. There was more abundance than ever. There was a greater sense of national pride, of American power on the international scene.

But for Black soldiers, the return was a daunting challenge. They had found acceptance despite their racial difference, both among their fighting comrades as well as by the natives of France, Italy, and other countries they helped liberate. After all, the war they were waging was to eradicate the fighting machines of national supremacists such as Hitler and Mussolini. The Americans were fighting for justice and equality, against the fascism of racial and ethnic hatred.

> But, upon their return, especially for Black soldiers coming back to the South, there was the shocking brutality of the same racism they thought they had conquered overseas.

One egregious example was emotionally stunning. You can sense that the Chauvin-Floyd case of 2020 has an eerie similarity to one that took place so many years before.

Returning as a decorated sergeant with three medals after serving for four years, twenty-three-year-old Isaac Woodard was returning home on February 12, 1946, hours after being honorably discharged, to his family in South Carolina. During the long trip, he had the need to use a restroom at one of the stops, but the bus driver denied him that privilege, demanding, "Boy, go sit back down!" and argued with him to remain on the bus, addressing him with insulting language. Strengthened by his experience as a respected man overseas, Woodard defied local tradition by standing up for himself and the driver finally agreed, but the hostile tone was set.

When the bus reached the town of Batesburg, the driver contacted the local police, who forcibly removed Woodard from the bus and began beating him. The police chief, Lynwood Shull, used his police billy club to beat him over the head and then gouge out Woodard's eyes, one by one, causing him to be blind for life. When Woodard was finally taken to a hospital, his medical diagnosis was "Bilateral Phthisis Bulbi of traumatic origin" and his prognosis characterized as "Hopeless."[1]

Woodard was put in jail for the night and taken to the local judge the next morning where he was found guilty of disturbing the peace and fined fifty dollars. When asked to speak for his defense, Woodard stated that he understood that he was beaten for saying "Yes" instead of "Yes, sir." This was documented when Chief Shull was eventually taken to court months later under the mandate of an angry President Harry S. Truman when this story was related to him.[2] Not surprisingly, the police chief was quickly acquitted by an all-White jury in less than a half-hour.

This belated trial of the police chief would not have occurred if the actor Orson Welles had not shone the light of media (radio) on this ugly event on July 28 of that year, and four subsequent broadcasts. That's what it took to seek justice in that racist culture at that historical era of Black history. Later that year, iconic folksinger Woody Guthrie wrote and performed the song, *The Blinding of Isaac Woodard*.

The outcome was not all bad. Following this shallow victory for racist practices, when Chief Shull was so quickly acquitted, President Truman learned of this story and reacted by establishing the Civil Rights Commission by Executive Order later that year. On July 29, 1947, Truman made a strong speech, declaring a "deep conviction that we have reached a turning point . . . to ensure that all Americans enjoy these rights." He looked out at the audience, paused for a couple of long moments and then added: "When I say all Americans—I mean all Americans."[3]

In July of 1948, Truman issued Executive Order 9981, banning racial discrimination in the US Army, and Executive Order 9980, integrating the federal government.

In 2018, Woodard's "drunk and disorderly" conviction was vacated, and a historical marker commissioned to commemorate the event in Carrollton, Georgia.[4] Yet in Minneapolis, Minnesota, nearly seventy-five years after Woodard was blinded by Chief Shull, history repeated itself and George Floyd was choked to death at the knee of police officer Derek Chauvin. But this time, the entire nation witnessed the troubling event through a video captured by a young bystander.

No Trust in Justice in the Age of Misinformation

Just weeks before the death of George Floyd, as I mentioned previously, there was the killing of Ahmaud Arbery in Georgia by the McMichaels, a father-and-son team, in an overeager attempt at making a citizen's arrest of an unarmed man just jogging down the street. And in the prior months and years, there were other accounts of White police officers violently attacking, sometimes killing, Black citizens. For example, police officer Jeronimo Yanez pulled over a young Black man, Philando Castile, during a traffic stop and when Castile mentioned, as was proper, that he was lawfully carrying a firearm in the car, the officer suddenly escalated the event and shot Castile though, as the video showed, he was complying totally with the officer's requests.

Then there was the case of in 2015 of a South Carolina police officer shooting unarmed Walter Scott in the back as he was running from a scuffle. When asked by a jury why he did this, officer Michael Slager replied, "I was scared," and that in his head, he felt "total fear."

And there's the infamous case of the unarmed teenager, Trayvon Martin, being killed by George Zimmerman when he decided that Martin "looks like he's up to no good" on a rainy night.

How did justice manifest itself in these cases? Juries acquitted both Yanez and Zimmerman. Slager ended up with a hung jury.

The victim of all this, beyond the people involved, was trust, a sense of trust in the world in which they lived, and now feared. Trust between White officers and Black young men. Trust between Black and

White citizens. According to an analysis of city data, the Minneapolis Police used force against its Black citizens seven times more frequently than against White people during the past five years. But this was not known to most citizens, not in this Age of Misinformation.

> Trust is fragile. It takes years to build and an instant to implode.

The Case for Police Reality

Now back to the night of May 28, 2020. The protesters in Minneapolis were expressing their frustration, anger, and fear. Hundreds and hundreds of protesters accumulated around the Third Precinct in the Longfellow neighborhood of Minneapolis. Now they were looting the nearby storefronts and setting fire to the building where the precinct was located. The police were nowhere to be seen at this point and reporters were openly asking why they weren't protecting life, limb, and property at such a crucial and critical time.

One could argue that the police had their issue with trust as well. Perhaps they feared for their own safety, if not lives, and feared that if they ended up hurting someone in their own self-defense, the courts could hold them responsible and criminally liable. The government leaders contributing to this decision to avoid showing up also lacked trust in the process, should violence result and they be held accountable. They feared lies being created to hold them liable, even though they were just trying to do their job. The fear was palpable.

The answers came slowly. There was a critical, strategic decision not to have police protect the neighborhood, including the precinct, because it was thought that the police presence would only instigate more violence and the probability of fatal conflict between police and protesters. All around, there was no shortage of mistrust in this Age of Misinformation.

Soon after ten that night, the Third Precinct was going up in flames, broadcast live on CNN, creating a surreal image of celebratory destruction as fireworks complemented the brilliant night flames, as if to commemorate the death of trust. It was like a Burning Man event run by the children from William Golding's *Lord of the Flies*.

Former officers told *The Minneapolis Star Tribune* that the police were upset with Mayor Jacob Frey's decision to abandon the Third Precinct station during the protests. Demonstrators set the building on fire after officers left. Protesters also hurled bricks and insults at officers. Numerous officers and protesters were injured.

A visibly tired and frustrated Minneapolis Mayor Jacob Frey made a first public appearance of the night early May 29th at City Hall. He took responsibility for what happened to the precinct, claiming it had become too dangerous for his officers.

The Case for Protester Reality

What were the protesters feeling, beyond the sense of injustice? What was sparking such an outburst of frustration? What was the context into which this conflagration arose? The larger context was the COVID-19 pandemic, causing a different kind of frustration—the need to deprive ourselves of normal social contact; to hide half our face with a mask in any social interaction; to avoid touching, let alone hugging, those we loved if we weren't living together; to wonder about every surface we touched when outside our homes. Then there were the results of the COVID virus and its quarantine, loss of jobs leading to the dilemma of no funds to pay rent, other bills, even feed oneself.

These protesters, many of them young and wired for social interaction, were frustrated even before the critical incident to which they were reacting. Some of them, people of color, were more likely to be victims of COVID-19, not only resulting in more deaths, but also in terms of loss of jobs and income.

These young people, some of them drawn to a seductive feeling of dominance as they confronted the establishment, represented by commercial business, both large and small, acted out and felt the brute power of smashing windows and looting stores, protected by the anonymity of the surging crowd. Perhaps it's possible they were led on by extremist agitators, from out of state.

Some of them were aware that many thousands of virus infections and consequent deaths might have been avoided had the government began quarantine protocols in January or February rather than March. More frustration! Less trust!

So, many a protester was reacting not only to the sense of injustice of White police over Black citizens but also to a sense of helplessness over their own lives, and the threat of death—their own and those of loved ones—because the decision about controlling a deadly virus invasion came too late.

Trust THIS!

No wonder they were frustrated. Though most of the protesters were law-abiding citizens and dutifully wearing their masks, there was that outlying group of wild, younger people who took the initiative to express that pervasive frustration, anger, and fear that all were feeling, deep down, with nowhere to express it. And, so, the Third Precinct went up in flames, as if to say: "Trust? Trust the police? Trust our government? Trust THIS!" as their erect middle fingers poked into the dark, burning night to declare their loss of faith in the experience of trust.

Deputy Chief Henry Halvorson said in an email to supervisors a few weeks after the incident that some officers had simply walked off the job without filing the proper paperwork, creating confusion about who was still working and who wasn't. There was no trust here either. The police felt that their perspective was not being recognized. "[Officers] don't feel appreciated," said Mylan Masson, a retired Minneapolis officer and use-of-force expert. "Everybody hates the police right now. I mean everybody."

US Rep. Ilhan Omar, a Minnesota Democrat who represented part of Minneapolis, told CNN's *State of the Union* that the Minneapolis Police Department was suffering a crisis of credibility [or trust] and needed to be dismantled.

When Alternate Realities Collide: And Another Killing—Followed by the "Blue Flu"

Then, just a few weeks later, two personalities collided, again a White police officer and a young, Black man. On the night of June 12, about ten o'clock, Officers Garett Rolfe and Devin Brosnan were called to check out a car parked at a Wendy's fast-food restaurant in Atlanta, blocking the parking area. In the car, fast asleep, was Rayshard Brooks. The police tapped on the window, asked Brooks to come out of his car, and interviewed him for about half an hour so Brooks could explain his situation. He was given a sobriety test that he failed, his blood alcohol level being a mere 0.03 over the legal limit.

Following the somewhat gentlemanly interview, during which Brooks was soft spoken and gentle in manner, Officer Rolfe changed the tone of the conversation and let Brooks know he was now going to be handcuffed and taken to jail for driving under the influence (DUI). Little did Rolfe know that Brooks was on probation, struggling to find a job to support his family of a wife, three daughters, and a stepson. This DUI charge, even without conviction, would mean going back to prison. Apparently, this was too much for Brooks who, at the last moment as he was about to be cuffed, decided to make a break for it.

Brooks' prior jail sentence was due to constraining someone against their will and for credit card fraud. In a recorded interview some time previous, he shared how challenging it was to find a job once there was a record of a conviction. He appeared sincere and authentic in his attempt to overcome his personal challenges but seemed on his way to personal accountability and a stable life, with the aim of supporting his young family.

Police officer Garrett Rolfe had a decent record and had taken trainings on the use of deadly force and on using de-escalation options at the DeKalb County police academy. But, when Brooks broke away and Rolfe began chasing him, things unfolded in a very unhappy manner. The two officers captured Brooks and took him to the ground, but Brooks, so fearful of returning to prison and not thinking rationally, broke free from the officers and grabbed Rolfe's Taser gun.

No doubt, after wrestling on the ground and unable to manage Brooks, Rolfe was not in a calm disposition. Chasing Brooks with the stolen Taser, Officer Rolfe reached for his pistol and shot at him three times, hitting him twice in the back. So great was his frustration, that Rolfe kicked at his body as Brooks lay struggling for his life, uttering, "Got him."

The next night, there were protests for this incident as well, resulting in the burning of the store at which the event took place and the burning of some nearby cars. Trust in the police system was dealt another devastating blow.

The day after, Atlanta Police Chief Erika Shields resigned, even though she had no direct involvement whatsoever in the incident. Had she lost trust in the police system as well?

A few days later, Fulton County District attorney Paul Howard, Jr. charged officer Rolfe with felony murder, five counts of aggravated assault, four police oath violations, and damage to property. The next day officers in the area avoided showing up at work, often claiming illness, known among the police as the "blue flu," a passive-aggressive form of protest. Now even the police had lost trust in the system.

The incidents described in this chapter reveal a striking theme of police with one agenda and point of view—policing their territory and keeping it safe from criminals—and the point of view of the citizens of color they serve, particularly the young, impoverished males, often fearful of police apprehension. Lazarus Daniel, a twenty-six-year-old meeting with former President Obama while being filmed on CNN, had this to say: "My biggest thing is making it back home regardless . . . regardless of the police. They don't know me from a can of paint."[5]

He went on to say how he was being pulled over almost nightly and typically asked if had any guns or drugs in the car, even though he was a devoted family man with no history of trouble with the police. Hearing his words helps us understand the apprehension many such young men feel about the police. For the most part, the police are just doing their job, though there occasionally appears to be some bias in place.

In many cases, the bias is on both sides. "War stories," both shared among police in their precincts, and among young males in the neighborhood, may contribute to biases against one another, and ultimately to alternate realities. Social media may strengthen such biases and both parties become victim to the possibilities of ongoing misinformation and exaggeration, one of the characteristics of the Age of Misinformation.

Taking Charge by Passing Laws that Tame Racism

One unexpected variant of the BLM movement, described more fully in the next chapter, is the anger aimed at Asians, culminating with the pandemic. Just a few short blocks from where I live, a twenty-one-year-old shooter killed eight people, six of them Asian women. Yet this harassment has a long history, just overshadowed by the BLM experience till recently.[6]

Yet there are still those who claim the BLM movement is based on a hoax, or a false reality, as put forth in books like *I Can't Breathe: How a Racial Hoax Is Killing America*[7] and *Race Crazy: BLM, 1619, and the Progressive Racism Movement*.[8] In *I Can't Breathe*, David Horowitz, a former leftist radical now turned against his former comrades, makes the argument that BLM is the biggest hoax of the twenty-first century. In *Race Crazy*, author Charles Love decries the significance of BLM, exposing it as a dangerous overreaction by the entertainment industry, corporate America, and the educational institutions, and undermining the notion of a united America. These are examples of recent books that counter the argument for allegiance to the BLM movement.

Then there are books that make the case against social injustice: *How We Can Win*,[9] *The Sum of Us*,[10] *All That She Carried*,[11] and *Just Pursuits* by CNN's own Laura Coates.[12] The battle of alternate realities continues.

A year after the George Floyd incident, changes were finally being made to curb the aggressive character of police enforcement against minorities. The State of Illinois, for example, rewrote the law, making accountability by police mandatory.[13] On a larger scale, over 140 new police reform laws were passed by thirty states.[14] Specifically, sixteen states restricted neck restraints, and four states limited officer immunity, among other changes.

On June 25, 2020, Congress passed the George Floyd Justice in Policing Act, establishing "a framework to prevent and remedy racial profiling by law enforcement at the federal, state, and local levels. It also limits the unnecessary use of force and restricts the use of no-knock warrants, chokeholds, and carotid holds."[15]

By 2022, there were significant changes in attitudes about traffic stops focusing on Black drivers, in part because of the growing awareness of how deadly some of these stops were becoming.[16] Cities like Los Angeles; Pittsburgh; Philadelphia; Seattle; Lansing, Michigan; and Brooklyn Center, Minnesota began restricting the policing of suspected minor violations. "There is a trust factor," Mayor Andy Schor of Lansing said in an interview, "that if you get pulled over—whether it's a moving violation, or pretextual, or whatever—you're not going to end up dead."[17]

As a matter of fact, for years prior, there was already a loss of confidence in the police action, particularly among Blacks. According to a report by the Gallup Poll of Annual Confidence in Institutions, while Whites scored a 56 percent confidence rating for police, Blacks scored only 19 percent.[18] Such low scores indicated a low point in how Blacks viewed police, especially when White police were acquitted after killing a Black man under arrest,[19] and would clearly benefit by the laws passed since then. Meanwhile, we have the brutal beating by five Black police officers of Tyre Nichols, a twenty-nine-year-old Black man just trying to get home to his mother.[20]

> In this chapter we could see more clearly how alternate realities, each with its own history of experience and rationale, can collide, with tragic outcomes.

Hopefully, the tears of grief will not be in vain if we can only learn to harness the power of listening across the cultural gap. Not only training but dialogue as well may help us conquer the stress of disinformation and take charge by bringing us to a common ground of mutual understanding and diminished fear—on both sides.

The confirmation of Judge Ketanji Brown Jackson by a Senate vote of fifty-three to forty-seven as the first Black woman to serve on the Supreme Court revealed a significant step in the march toward social equality in the history of the nation.[21]

"I stand on the shoulders of generations past who never had anything close to this opportunity" she proclaimed at her confirmation hearings. "This is a moment that all Americans should be proud."[22]

At a celebration of her confirmation a day later, she said, with tears in her eyes, "It has taken 232 years and 115 prior appointments for a Black woman to be selected to serve on the Supreme Court of the United States, but we've made it. We've made it, all of us."[23]

CHAPTER FOUR

For and against the BLM Movement: a Coming Civil War?

The cultural civil war that has been simmering underneath the surface is now boiling.

—Ben Domenech, publisher of *The Federalist*

We're in a twenty-first-century version of the Civil War.

—Rob Reiner, filmmaker

We decided to put on our [graduation] robes to show that there is Black excellence in our community. We walked the streets as our stage and protested.

—High school graduate Datelle Straub

During the George Floyd protests, a grid of broken windows, ransacked stores, and burned-out buildings marked the consequences of random crimes throughout Minneapolis. Videos could be seen of various people running in and out of stores, their arms filled with boxes of packaged items.

The events of the following days and nights added more fuel to the fire. There was no more graphic image than this to illustrate the loss of trust adding to the Black Lives Matter movement, aimed at restoring empathy and justice to minority groups of all kinds, but primarily Blacks. This began back in 2013 with a tweet by Alicia Garza about the killing of Trayvon Martin, an unarmed Black teenager by a fake security guard in Florida.

I take that back. There is another graphic image that is even more powerful: the open casket of fourteen-year-old Emmett Till, his bloated, battered face rendering him beyond recognition. The infamous account of his kidnap, brutal beating, and killing is well known, culminating in the 2022 film, *Till*.

Leaving his home in Chicago, Emmett was visiting his relatives in a town called Money in deep-South Mississippi in the summer of 1955. A highly spirited and jubilant personality, Emmett was warned about keeping a low profile during his visit but, nonetheless, while buying some goodies at a local store on August 24, he nonchalantly whistled at the owner's wife, Carolyn Bryant—something that would have hardly raised an eyebrow in Chicago. But in the hamlet of Money, that was an unforgivable act of defiance against the unwritten code of conduct for Blacks.

Emmett was kidnapped in the middle of the night four days later, beaten mercilessly, and shot through the head before being dumped into the Tallahatchie River, weighted down by a heavy cotton-gin fan tied to his neck with barbed wire.

When his mother, Mamie, finally got to see her son's mutilated body, she could see through the hole in his head made by the bullet that killed him from one temple through to the other—a hole clean enough to see the world through it. This became a metaphor for her insistence that the casket remain open for the rest of the world to see how a Black person could be treated, typically without consequence to the killers in the deep South.

A trial was held a few weeks later, trying Roy Bryant and his half brother, J.W. Milam, for murder. But an all-White, all-male jury took just enough time to refresh themselves with Coca-Cola before rendering a not-guilty verdict.

After nearly 200 attempts at legislation, President Biden finally passed the Emmet Till Anti-Lynching Act in the presence of Rev. Wheeler Parker, a surviving cousin of Emmett Till.

> This nadir in social injustice brought to a head the need for recognition that Black lives really do matter.

Sixty-seven years later, the echoes of Emmett's death rang ruefully in cities like Richmond, Virginia; Reno, Nevada; Philadelphia, Pennsylvania; Los Angeles, California; Salt Lake City, Utah; Minneapolis, Minnesota; and Washington, DC.

Loss of Trust in Protesters

Later in the summer of 2020, protests starting with George Floyd's killing escalated and spread throughout the country. With masks hanging loosely on their chins and social distancing forgotten in the heat of the moment, protesters—some called them rioters—smashed windows at the police building in Richmond, Virginia; and set fire to the city hall in Reno, Nevada. In Philadelphia, thirteen officers were seriously wounded, and four police vehicles vandalized when an initially peaceful protest turned ugly. In Los Angeles, police used rubber bullets to keep the crowds at bay after they had ransacked the expensive boutiques along the popular shopping neighborhood at Fairfax and Melrose as a graffiti-covered police car burned in the night. In Salt Lake City, one police car was overturned and another set ablaze as one officer was hospitalized after being hit in the head with a bat.

In Minneapolis, the epicenter of it all, 4,000 National Guard troops were called in to quell the fearsome events of the previous nights. Governor Tim Walz was quoted as saying that this was no longer a civil protest, but rather "about attacking civil society, instilling fear, and disrupting our great cities."

In Washington, DC, Secret Service agents, aided by the US Park Police and National Guard troops, were busy keeping the crowds at bay, pushing them back to Lafayette Park and Pennsylvania Avenue, as they attacked and looted businesses in the blocks surrounding the White House.

Toward the end of that first week, over 1,300 individuals were arrested in sixteen cities across the nation, 500 in Los Angeles on a single Friday night.

Returning from his visit to Florida to witness the SpaceX rocket launch, President Trump ignored the journalists and made his way to the White House.

Inside the Killer Mind

What makes this age of reporting different from that of the last generation's is the ubiquitous presence of surveillance opportunities, primarily by personal cell phones, as well as the body cameras worn by more and more police officers. Controversies between police and citizens can now be more accurately seen and reported. The iconic video of the George Floyd, knee-in-the-neck incident was taken by a bystander—not a reporter and not a police officer. Police videos did not appear.

That video, with its soundtrack including the plea, "Mama," struck at the heart strings of all who have a scintilla of empathy in their soul, and the statement, "I can't breathe," as Officer Chauvin continued his knee-hold, defied any logic as to why the knee was not removed at that time. *Mama* and *I can't breathe* became the mottos of many a protester.

Those soldiers who have had comrades killed in combat may be familiar with the surprising call for a mother's assistance as they are facing death. It is an irrational yet reflexive final call for saving grace in such dire straits—the primal expression of our need to trust. This intimate call for help indicates a great deal about Floyd as well as about Chauvin as he must have heard Floyd in this moment of utter vulnerability. Anyone with any compassion at all would have responded and tried to help the man instead of continuing to hold him down.

One can't help but wonder what was going through Chauvin's mind at the time. How could he not know he was using unnecessary force? How could he not know he was causing this presumably innocent Black man extreme distress, at the least? Was he intentionally trying to cause duress to Floyd? It turns out that Officer Chauvin had a history of difficulties in his file. Three years earlier, there was a report of his practicing the exact same thing against a woman who tried to use sarcasm to save herself from this abuse. "He just stayed on my neck," ignoring her desperate pleas to get off, Ms. Code said. Frustrated and upset, she challenged him to press harder. "Then he did. Just to shut me up," she said. Although this was one of six similar cases reported against Officer Chauvin as far back as 2015, he was never formally reprimanded until the George Floyd incident.

Maya Santamaria, former owner of El Nuevo Rodeo club, knew Chauvin while he was working there off-time for seventeen years as a bouncer, as tending to overreact to Black individuals, and not doing so with Latino individuals. "I thought he would have more of a conscience," she said about the infamous incident. "Even if he is a bit of racist, he's a human being . . . At what point does your humanity overpower your racial bias?"

Chauvin was charged with third-degree murder, then later changed to second-degree murder, and second-degree manslaughter when the medical examiner found that Floyd's death was a homicide that happened because of "a cardiopulmonary arrest while being restrained by law enforcement officer(s)."

We might also wonder why any of the other three officers, Thomas Lane, S. Alexander Kueng, and Tou Thao, did not persuade Chauvin to release their prisoner so he could breathe. Were they afraid of Chauvin? Did they think they would get into an uncomfortable disagreement with him? What kind of presumed authority did Chauvin have over the other officers to the extent that they did not intervene? Did they fear overreaction on his part? Did they not trust him to take their recommendations? There is also the possibility that they did not know or did not care that Mr. Floyd was being hurt. One can't help but recall footage of Nazi officers in World War II exerting unnecessary force against their prisoners just out of sheer hatred. I hesitate to compare Chauvin to those Nazi soldiers, but I can't think of an excuse for him, either.

No Trust in Masks

On TV, former President Trump made a comment about the fact that the police deserted the 3rd Precinct building and let it burn. He seemed to think it should have been defended and that the people in charge just didn't care. However, that police department probably did not, at the time, have the resources needed to defend it. In any case, Milwaukee Police Chief Alfonso Morales was fired in early August of 2020 by a unanimous vote of the city's Fire and Police Commission when numerous issues arose over his handling of the Black communities in the city.

Among the protesters were those who were already frustrated and angry about the pandemic. They were tired of being told to stay home and avoid congregating in groups. They were already starting to think that maybe the government was exaggerating the problem just to exert control over them in a dictatorial manner—lack of trust. Several statements on Fox News and other places opined that some of the state governors were being unreasonable, even acting like dictators. Perhaps they were going too far. Indeed, some of the arrests were absurd, such as arresting a man in a boat out on a lake for fishing. He wasn't exposing anyone or himself to danger. There was a report that Mayor Richard Montgomery of Manhattan Beach in California told people they could go out on the beach so long as they were on "wet sand" but couldn't get on "dry sand." At what point do the rules become ridiculous?

People were turning on their friends and neighbors for violations of the rules, i.e., not staying six feet part, congregating in groups, not wearing masks. Even worse, individuals were starting to distrust one another. If someone wasn't wearing a mask in public, they were subject to verbal abuse and shame and told they were being selfish by exposing others.

There were many who actively resisted the mask-wearing requirement. Some were pushing back by intentionally not wearing a mask in public to show their defiance of the government. "It is unconstitutional to make people wear masks," some said. Interviewed at a beach, one young man replied, "If the president doesn't want to wear a mask, then that's good enough for me."

Another said to a TV reporter before an indoor Trump rally on Sept. 13, "I'm not gonna let a government tell me what to do." Some were thinking that "this whole pandemic thing" was a government attempt to control people and get them to comply so they could exert more tyrannical control and take away their constitutional rights. They were clearly demonstrating more mistrust of government.

A divide developed between those who wore their masks religiously and those who avidly defended their freedom not to, not only in the US but in Europe as well. In the United Kingdom, for instance, Camilla Long wrote in *The Sunday Times* that the rule to wear masks "makes no sense, another exercise in dreary conformity."[1] One lawmaker in London called masks a "monstrous imposition," as British leaders confused their citizenry with unclear directives.

Losing Trust in Trump

One couple in Las Vegas had a six-year-old daughter and a one-year-old baby. The husband, Mark, worked many hours a day at a computer company, so he wasn't home much to babysit. The wife, Monica, was shopping with her girls. A lady who was also shopping told her, "You can be arrested for child abuse for bringing your children shopping with you, exposing them to the virus."

"Oh," said Monica, "then I'm supposed to leave them home alone? That's okay?"

Some of the younger people were upset with the government but didn't know where or how to place the blame for their anger. Monica was the manager of a restaurant. She had not worked since the beginning of the lockdown and didn't know when the restaurant would reopen. She blamed the government and President Trump because she didn't know what else to do with her anger. Again, a lack of trust that many young people shared.

President Trump had his own trust issues. In his speeches he could be seen blaming Communist China for withholding information on the virus and allowing people to travel when they knew the virus was highly contagious. He also blamed the World Health Organization for taking China's viewpoint and deceiving the world about the danger of the virus—hence, his decision to withhold funds from the WHO. When he was confronted with the lies revealed by Bob Woodward, he merely shot back at the author for not disclosing the truth when he had it before publication of the book. Here again was a lack of trust, however it may be justified, with great economic repercussions that would result from this breach of trust.

Did President Trump trust his governors? This is what he had to say after the fact, according to *The New York Times*: "You have to dominate," he told them. "If you don't dominate, you're wasting your time—they're going to run over you, you're going to look like a bunch of jerks."

In his book, *Surviving Autocracy*, Masha Gerson referred to Trump as a "Styrofoam President running a Government of Destruction with Power Lies." According to Gerson, Trump viewed power as dominance. He used tweets, provocative and incendiary, as a way of radicalizing people rather than uniting them. Gerson holds Trump responsible for the death of dignity and characterizes his leadership approach as "aspirational autocracy."[2]

In response to all the reaction against the killing of George Floyd, President Trump decided to retaliate in his own manner. In the heat of the protests, he decided to act in a typical Trumpian manner. His ordered that the protesters be forcefully removed from the vicinity of the White House with the presumed necessity to clear the area so he and his staff could walk to St. John's Church around the corner across Lafayette Park for what turned out to be a photo op, an expression of religious righteousness against the supposed aggressiveness of the protesters. After the protesters were physically pushed away by the police, he and his staff walked briskly to the church where Trump awkwardly held up a Bible, his lips crimped with mixed message, wondering possibly, if people would fall for this fake image.

General John Allen, former commander of the US Forces in Afghanistan, declared how much he prized First Amendment rights to speak freely and was critical of Trump's decision to clear the area in front of the White House forcibly despite the calm nature of the protesters. All this for a clumsy photo op in front of St. John's Episcopal Church. Former Secretary of State Colin Powell, in an interview with Fareed Zakaria, stated that Trump was just criticizing anyone who didn't agree with him, lied all the time and that the "country is getting wise to this and we're not going to put up with it anymore." He wondered if the thousands of protesters present that day indicated that we were at a turning point.

No Trust for First Amendment Rights

The incident of the CNN reporter and his camera crew became significant and even iconic. This was in Minneapolis not long after the protests began. Omar Jimenez was arrested while explaining that he was a reporter while the camera was still running. The reporter immediately showed his identification, so there was no excuse to arrest him. He politely asked why he was being arrested and was told by one of the officers that he was "following orders." (He never found out whose orders, nor did anyone else.) Jimenez cooperated politely and was held in a police van for about an hour. The then CEO of CNN, Jeff Zucker, was notified, called the governor and, after an hour of waiting in the van, the reporter was released. Governor Tim Walz issued a public apology, admitting that this was "a clear violation of ... First Amendment rights."

Such incidents contribute to the public loss of trust. A White reporter, John Campbell, was questioned by police about the same time but not arrested. He later commented that he was treated better than Jimenez, a Black reporter. One cannot prove discrimination based on skin color, but it certainly does raise questions. This was a violation of the constitutional right of the free press. As more and more constitutional rights were being violated—to say nothing of people's lives being upset and property being destroyed—more and more, trust was becoming a failure of hope.

A Coming Civil War

In Brooklyn, a police officer on an antilooting patrol was attacked from behind with a knife just before midnight by an assailant. In the struggle that followed, two other officers were slightly injured with gunshot injuries to their hands. When they ended up in a hospital, Police Commissioner Dermot Shea remarked, "Are we surprised? Are we surprised we're here in the hospital again? Did we doubt because of the rhetoric we're hearing, the antipolice rhetoric that's storming our streets, are we surprised that we got this call? I'm not."

As it became evident, there were individuals who had their own agenda—chaos, rather than protest. Federal agents had arrested three men, Stephen T. Parshall, Andrew Lynam, and William Loomis who, police believed, were planning to disrupt a Black Lives Matter protest in Las Vegas. They faced federal charges of conspiracy, possession of unregistered firearms, and multiple terrorism-related state charges. Prosecutors said that the men were planning to use explosives and firebombs to create turmoil and panic that would lead to havoc. "The goal would be to set the devices off and cause panic to the police and public, in hopes that it caused others to take some type of action," according to the complaint. "Whether it be by police or by the public, Lynam and Parshall wanted some type of confrontation between the police and protesters." It appeared that there was no trust lost between these hooligans and the protesters with higher moral values.

All three, who are White and had US military experience, "self-identified as part of the 'boogaloo' movement," a disparate group including radical gun rights activists, far-right militias, neo-Nazis, and White supremacists. As mentioned in the criminal complaint, "Boogaloo is a term used by extremists to signify a coming civil war or fall of civilization."

This was concrete evidence of the role played by radicals in some of the destruction and violence in otherwise peaceful demonstrations over the weeks of protest, seeking to exploit otherwise peaceful events to advance their role in taking down the US government.

"There is no doubt that there are people who use this moment to steal," said New York Governor Andrew Cuomo on June 5. "These are people who will exploit that moment . . . try to color the whole process."

All this back-and-forth dynamic between peaceful protesters and "extremist groups who are using this for their own purpose" leading to "rightful outrage," according to Gov. Cuomo, was leading to "a nation that is more divided than at any point in my life. People see this moment and they exploit it . . . two different motivations—there is no comparison between the two."

"If there is no trust," he said a few days later, "the community is not going to allow the police to police. Let's get to a table and let everyone say their piece."

Sometime later, Chris Larsen, a veteran techie and crypto currency mogul, decided to install surveillance cameras in the San

Francisco area. Why? He saw placing cameras around the city as a way of enlisting the assistance of neighborhood citizens to help build trust in the community. According to a press statement, "Mr. Larsen argues that trust will come in the form of full city camera coverage, so the police can play a smaller, more subtle role. Individual vigilantism will not work, he argued, but strong neighborhoods with continuous video feeds on every corner will."

No Trust between Us and Them

In July, President Trump decided to employ federal troops, mostly border police, to "come to the aid" of cities such as Portland and Seattle to aid in the control of protesters. But now these troops themselves became the focus of protesters.

In Portland, on the evening of July 25 and reaching into the early hours of the following day, protesters clashed with federal officers near a courthouse. The protesters began gathering after nine o'clock that evening and continued the confrontation beyond two thirty the following morning. Canisters of teargas were lobbed at the protesters, some of whom just picked them up and tossed them back at the police. The attorney general of Oregon requested a halt to the influx of federal police, but a federal judge denied that request.

On July 25, despite the protests of Seattle's mayor, Jenny Durkan, and Police Chief Carmen Best, federal agents were deployed there to protect federal buildings. Rocks and bottles were thrown at local officers. Over forty-five protesters were arrested for assaulting officers, failing to disperse, and damaging property when a device, lobbed into a police station, was said to have "exploded."

That same night, in Austin, Texas, twenty-eight-year-old Garrett Foster, a protester carrying a rifle, was shot to death by a driver in a car traveling through the crowd as Foster approached the car. Foster was the sole caretaker of his fiancée, Whitney Mitchel, who had her four limbs amputated due to illness. Texas is an open carry state where firearms can legally be carried in public. Ironically, Foster was a Caucasian, and his fiancée is African American. One wonders what their level of trust was when it came to race relations and what brought them to the protest rally.

By early August, there was still violence in certain areas. In Chicago, over a hundred people were arrested for breaking windows, looting stores, and fighting with police on the Magnificent Mile, Chicago's premier shopping area. "In many neighborhoods," according to *The New York Times*, "gun violence has been unrelenting, soaring to levels not seen in decades."[3]

Only weeks later, on August 23, another incident led to even more protests. In the city of Kenosha, Wisconsin, police shot Jacob Blake in the back at least seven times as he walked around the front of his car, followed by the police. With three of his children in the car, it is unlikely that Mr. Blake was intending any threat to the police and so the protesters felt justified in their efforts to eradicate systemic racism. Blake survived the shooting but will be paralyzed below the waist for life.[4]

A few days later, on the third night of the Kenosha protest following Jacob Blake's shooting, seventeen-year-old Kyle Rittenhouse, armed with an assault rifle, killed two protesters—Anthony Huber and Joseph Rosenbaum—while also injuring Gaige Grosskreutz, in the downtown commercial area of Kenosha during a conflict. Voices could be heard: "He just shot someone. He just shot someone." Witnesses described him as vigilante militia though he was casually attired. He was seen arguing with protesters before the murders. Rosenbaum was seen chasing him. Democratic State Senator David Bower was concerned about White supremacists coming in from surrounding cities and Milwaukee radio reporter Tony Atkins was shocked by "a whole new violent scenario."[5,6]

Trust, whether between protesters and hooligans,[7] between police and citizenry,[8] between political parties,[9] between Trump and "undesirable" immigrants,[10] between the Trump administration and victims of COVID-19,[11] between *us* and *them*, is running on empty. What ever happened to our need to trust? And now we have a president who is willing to stand up to the task at hand. "Advancing equity has to be everyone's job," Biden said soon after being inaugurated. "We must change. I know it's going to take time. But I firmly believe that the nation is ready to change . . . We need to make the issue of racial equality . . . to be the business of the whole government."[12]

One of the solutions is to improve the overall approach of police interaction with sincere protesters. A report by the New York City Department of Investigation recommended having a more centralized strategy to avoid confusing messages that could just accelerate aggressive interaction on both sides, and to exercise a greater sense of proportionality depending on any given context. The report went on to say that there was a strong need for more training of officers and that a militarized approach was not always appropriate[13] *The New York Times* called it "a startling display of violence and disarray," blaming "lack of training" and overuse of aggressive force.[14] By the middle of 2022, the NYPD had hit a twenty-eight-year high in gun arrests, collecting over 3,000 guns.[15]

When the attacks on Asians became more prominent in the press, it became apparent that they had grown exponentially in 2020, possibly caused by Trump referring to COVID-19 as the "Chinese virus," according to a survey done at San Bernardino.[16]

At the bottom of this issue of continuing violence and gun attacks was the availability of firearms, both pistols and long guns, to young people, who could legally buy firearms at the age of eighteen and then use them to kill the same day, as did Payton Gendron in Buffalo and Michael Louis in Tulsa in the summer of 2022.

Biden had had enough and lamented the "killing fields" as Congress did little to limit gun sales. He demanded laws to limit the sales of assault weapons.[17]

Voices from the Past

Though the BLM movement began in mid-2013 and continued to grow as more Blacks were being killed by White police through the following decade, the roots of racial discrimination go back centuries. Because of the graphic nature of the injustice of the murder of Floyd as it was being digitally recorded by various onlookers for more than ten minutes, there was a growing focus on the movement that lasted months and months, but gradually lost momentum. We can easily forget the long history of racial discrimination against Blacks in America if we take our eyes away from those scenes. But there were recordings of another nature that took place to verify a much more deliberate manifestation of racism—oral records.

To finish off this chapter, I can do no better than quote the following author on his experience of visiting the National Museum of African American History and Culture in Washington, DC.

On a rainy Thursday afternoon in November, best-selling author Clint Smith, writing for the *Federal Writers' Project*, stepped inside the museum. On past visits, he shared, he'd always encountered crowds of tourists. But on this day, the museum was nearly empty. His account is so touching that it's worth reading verbatim:

> I made my way down to the bottom level, which documents the history of slavery in America. Masks were mandatory, and something about the pieces of cloth covering everyone's mouths seemed to amplify the silence and solemnity of what surrounded us.
>
> I walked past the statue of Thomas Jefferson standing among bricks bearing the names of people he'd enslaved, past a cabin that enslaved people had slept in, and past the stone auction block upon which enslaved people had been sold and separated from their families.
>
> Toward the end of a long corridor was a dimly lit room with sepia-toned photos on the walls. Photos of enslaved

people holding their own children, or their enslaver's children. Photos of fresh wounds on the backs of those who'd been beaten. Photos of people bent over fields of cotton that hid their faces.

But what was most striking about the room was the voices running through it. The words of people who had survived slavery were running on a six-minute loop. Their voices floated through the air like ghosts.

"My father was not allowed to see my mother but two nights a week," said a woman in the voice of Mary A. Bell. "Dat was Wednesday and Saturday. So he often came home all bloody from his beatings."

"I had to wok evva day," said a woman in the voice of Elvira Boles. "I'd leave mah baby cryin' in the yard, and I'd be cryin', but I couldn't stay."

"My mudder work in de field," said Harrison Beckett. "Sometimes she come in nine or ten 'clock at night. She be all wore out an' it be so dark she too tired to cook lots of times, but she hafter git some food so we could eat it. Us all 'round de table like dat was like a feast."[18]

RADICAL STRATEGIES: OUR RESPONSE TO RACIAL INJUSTICE

Systemic

- **Affirmation:** Affirm and acknowledge the values that allow each of us to take pride in our heritage without demeaning other races.

Community

- **Support:** Create a strong sense of support in communities exposed to racism. Validating others' experiences in small circle groups requires emotional awareness, empathy, and sincerity. It's crucial to ensure that this opportunity not be abused by those just seeking attention, but rather coming to the table with sincerity and a genuine intent to share and listen. This process may require third party support by facilitators with training in this skill, so that both participants and observers can better trust the integrity of the outcome. When possible, these community-based meetings can be held at schools or colleges; faith-based settings—churches, temples; work settings such as corporations, police departments, or the Centers for Disease Control and Prevention; or social clubs like Kiwanis and Rotary.
- **Recognition:** Recognize the pervasive occurrence of unconscious or implicit racial bias that everyone brings to the table, both Whites and minority groups. This includes the polarized dynamics of tribalism, the *we-they* division that has grown to challenging proportions over the past administration.

Support groups and circles mentioned above apply here as well.

- **Sharing:** In order to preempt the hurt and anger arising out of racist experiences, and subsequently generated into intense outbursts disguised as legitimate protest, initiate opportunities for those deeply affected by racism to effectively communicate their experience of pain in larger group settings such as town-hall meetings, facilitated by community leaders, both White and minority. Social media can convey the process to illustrate how racist attitudes, both overt and implicit, can be dealt with and resolved with mutual respect.

- **Storytelling:** Storytelling is a powerful force for communicating racist experiences to others to help understand the personal pain involved, with all its subtle nuances. An effective story can focus on systemic historical aspects; community-based incidents; or individual, personal accounts. An effective story can have:
    - ☐ a beginning which introduces the storyteller and illustrates the innocence of experience that does not yet recognize how racism can hurt so deeply as the years go by
    - ☐ a middle that reveals the conflict experienced over time and the awareness that grows as one matures
    - ☐ and an ending that declares how individuals can claim their right to self-respect and ethnic pride with a call to action.
    - ☐ The skill of storytelling is one that can be structured and taught, especially by national organizations, such as The Moth, based in New York City; and the HubSpot Academy's free online Power of Storytelling course. As well, there are such sites as The Ultimate

Guide to Storytelling by Allie Decker, for starters.

- ☐ Storytellers are encouraged to share not only their experiences, but their emotions as well. Humor is encouraged if that fits comfortably into the speaker's natural style. Discussions can follow each story, with a give-and-take that all participants can enjoy.
- ☐ Storytelling can be community-based, performed at various sites, and shared through social media to carry messages across the country, as described in the above paragraphs.

Individual

- Self-esteem: The development of self-esteem as an aspirational goal is one of the components of the "pursuit of happiness" that the Declaration of Independence promises. Self-esteem is required for the development of trusting relationships which, in turn, can lead to the recognition and defeat of racism. All the above responses to racism can lead to greater self-esteem among individuals to help combat social injustice in all its diverse forms.

SECTION III:

SCORCHED

CRISIS IN CLIMATE CHANGE

CHAPTER FIVE

Scorched: Climate Change to Climate Crisis

We're not just ruining the world—we're destroying it.

—Sir David Attenborough, on *60 Minutes*

Once the climate has got your attention, you can't look away.

—Greta Thunberg

We are treating nature like a toilet... Humanity seems hell-bent on destruction... We are waging war on nature.

—UN Secretary-General António Guterres at UN Biodiversity Conference, Dec. 6, 2022

Urgency.
About overfishing our oceans and dying corals.

Urgency!
About burning down our forests, leading to global warming.

URGENCY!
About turning a blind eye to the accelerating rate of destruction of our planet.

*U*rgency is the best single word that describes the existential threat of climate change occurring in our time. To many aware of the situation, it's almost too late. Hopefully not. But the threat is clearly immediate.

According to a British documentary featuring David Attenborough, there are a million species at risk of extinction because of climate warming, threatening our food and water security and putting us at greater risk for future pandemics.

> Extinction of animals, plants, and fish, according to the report, are now occurring at one hundred times the rate of normal evolutionary patterns.

The key drivers are primarily biodiversity loss, including overfishing, climate change, and pollution. Up to 75 percent of Earth's surface has been shorn of its natural forest growth and transformed to use for agriculture and logging, robbing Earth of its global natural forest land, which function as the planet's lungs in keeping the CO_2 level down.[1]

"The ocean's mammals are at a crucial crossroads," say the biodiversity experts. A quarter of these species—which include whales, dolphins, seals, sea lions, manatees, dugongs, sea otters, and polar bears—are now classified as being at risk of extinction.[2]

According to the Goddard Institute for Space Studies, the mean temperature of the planet has increased by almost two degrees Celsius over the past 140 years.[3]

Whom to Trust?

In 2020, we had over a million acres of forest burn up and threaten major cities in northern California and Oregon, filling the air with smoke that drifted thousands of miles. During that year's hurricane season, we had more tropical storms make landfall than in any single season ever before.

Yet there are those who ask us to trust them when they proclaim that climate change is a hoax. Five hundred scientists across the globe want us to believe that the Little Ice Age ended as recently as 1850, thereby explaining the rise of temperatures we're now experiencing.[4] In a publication sent to the United Nations, they claim that current models are inadequate, "not remotely plausible as policy tools," and that "they most likely exaggerate the effect of greenhouse gases such as CO_2." Finally, they conclude, "There is no statistical evidence that global warming is intensifying hurricanes, floods, droughts, and suchlike natural disasters, or making them more frequent."[5]

There are many other scientists as well as politicians who strongly insist that climate change is a figment of our imagination. Here are the claims they make:

1) **Claim:** Climate change is all part of a natural cycle. They "prove" their case by looking at very short time periods, where occasional cooler weather disproves the warming aspect.

    Truth: Consistent scientific observations over the past forty years are too significant to deny.

2) **Claim**: Climate change just means we, and nature, must adjust just a little bit. There's no real problem.

    Truth: More and more land is constantly being developed, leaving nature blindsided. More and more creatures must continue migrating to survive higher temperatures. In addition, certain organisms, kept from overgrowing by cold winters, are now devastating their prey because their numbers are so high. At Jasper National Park, mountain pine beetles lay their eggs in the bark of pine trees and their larvae eat through the channels that supply nutrients to the trees, killing them in as little as two to four weeks. It takes several days of freezing temperatures to kill the bugs. This is happening less frequently over time, resulting in devastation of the forests, as well as the dead trees increasing the risk of fire. By 2019, about 98 percent of the pine trees at the National Park were infested. Ecological systems are very intricately connected, and temperature increases destroy the delicate balance. The trees act as the lungs of our planet and this function is being powerfully diminished. Also, when trees die, half their dead weight is released as carbon. Even if we try to replant the trees, in the first decade of a tree's life, it releases more CO_2 than it takes in.

3) **Claim:** How can there be warmer climates when it seems to be raining more frequently?

   Truth: Warmer temperatures result in more water evaporation, leading to more clouds and more rain. A study of Libyan weather patterns over the past 10,000 years has proven this to be true.

4) **Claim:** The models used to predict weather patterns are unreliable.

   Truth: Models are not perfect predictors. They depend on historical data. No one can perfectly predict the future.

5) **Claim:** There's no scientific consensus, not enough agreement.

   Truth: The media portray conflict among scientists to create drama. The truth is that there is an overwhelming consensus among climate scientists but there are always some who want to be deniers and they're the ones who get attention on the media.

Conspiracy theories tend to contradict reality that is based on scientific consensus. There are many reasons for that. As TV journalist, Fareed Zakaria, puts it, a simple lie is much easier to believe than a complex reality. Conspiracy theories tend to dramatize as they create false stories. But objective data always trump conspiracy theories, even if it takes a bit of time.

The truth is that temperatures in the far northern latitudes, such as Edmonton, Alberta in Canada, have already risen 1.7 degrees C over the past eighty years, and glaciers to the north are melting away at an increasingly faster rate.

> Even if the temperatures do not increase any further, 30 to 40 percent of all glaciers will be lost—forever.

The forest fires in California aren't going away as temperatures rise. On November 8, 2018, as 209,000 acres were burning, the town of Paradise was completely devastated. Its 27,000 residents were lucky to make it out of the roaring flames, though eighty-six perished.

Sometimes a little change in temperature can cause great damage. For example, a one degree rise in temperature over bodies of water can result in a 7 percent increase in rate of vaporization, leading to a significant increase in downpours. A 2 percent warming of the ocean can result in a 90 percent loss of coral life, consequently affecting an entire food chain for marine survival. But then there are the relatives and friends who have different opinions.

Here is a sample. A friend of mine, whose opinion I value highly and who stays abreast of the news, had this to say in one of his emails:

"If we really have such a dire overall warming pattern, then we would have warm winters too. If Earth were warming that much there would be records set everywhere, and not at a couple of spots from time to time (which is expected and normal). Weather changes, and it is normal to go from cold to hot to cold, etc. . . . like any kind of real or hyped-up 'emergency' to attract readers and sell commercials. Anyway, the fact is that the current warming trend is 0.03 degrees F per year, which because of hugely greater weather fluctuations, is absolutely imperceptible, and only detectable with very precise scientific instruments and lots of statistics over long periods of time."

Where Have All the Snow Slopes Gone?

Forty-four million years ago, the Alpine mountains formed the beautiful Alps that graze the edges of Switzerland and Italy. They were the consequence of two geological plates confronting one another—the European and the African. The collision kept them growing higher and higher and, until about nine million years ago, covered in snow and ice.

Over the past fifty years, the snow line in Europe has begun to recede, making the snow season shorter by almost a month. By December of 2020, geologists recorded the driest season in 150 years of record. The snow was down to 20 percent of its typical depth. And the temperature? Don't ask. But, if you did, I'd have to tell you that it was up to sixty-eight degrees F in the formerly cold winter skiing season in Gstaad, Switzerland![6] Despite attempts at filling the absence of snow with snowmaking machines, if the temperature remains below freezing, it just ain't the same.

Instead of enjoying the challenges of snow-filled slopes reaching as far as the eye can see, there are drab pathways of artificial snow next to a landscape of dried grass and scrub. This is one illustration of what climate change is doing to our fragile planet.

Two Alternate Realities of One World: Which Do You Trust?

Two views of one world: the hoax subscribers insist that there is no such thing as climate warming, rather just part of a series of cycles that our planet traverses. The others accept the science that is certain that we are indubitably going in a direction that is frighteningly close to the point of no return, where one climatic disaster after another is leading us into a planetary catastrophe, when millions of people living close to the coast of any country will be forced to flee.

Whom to believe in this conspiracy of trust? In this past

administration, Trump and his cronies defied science and bellowed as loudly as they could that all this stuff about climate change was simply a hoax. Trump rejected the Paris Agreement and contradicted even his own officials whenever they tried to warn him about the disastrous consequences of inattention to this grave matter.

He and his associates refused to acknowledge how our oceans were warming up and unable to continue absorbing as much CO_2 as they were able to in the past. As part of Earth's regulating system, the oceans were able to absorb both CO_2 and heat, helping moderate changes that were taking place even as the Industrial Revolution continued to belch more and more fossil fuel exhaust into our atmosphere.

Why did the former administration deny climate change, calling it a hoax? Perhaps Greta Thunberg has some insight into this. "People are suffering, people are dying, entire ecosystems are collapsing. We are in the beginning of a mass extinction and all you can talk about is money and fairytales of eternal economic growth."

Then, she added, in her 2021 PBS documentary, "So many people come up to me and say they believe that there's something wrong with them because they are feeling like shit. But I think it's the opposite. It's the rest who can maintain living in this society where we only care about prestige, and these are shallow things that don't matter, and being the best and so on. Those are the people who are not normal." She characterized the climate crisis as a "communication crisis," and in her humble manner concluded, "I don't want you to listen to me. I want you to listen to the science—before it's too late."[7]

Other words of wisdom from this very wise teenager: "The time for small steps is long gone," and "I get shocked every single day . . . when people don't connect the dots."

So, which alternate reality are we to believe and trust?

Can We Trust These Scenarios?

Climate warming is hardly a new discovery. In 1827, John Fourier had already written about the greenhouse effect. In 1896, Svante Arrhenius predicted that carbon dioxide in the atmosphere would raise the global temperature by four to six degrees Celsius. Current estimates, based on much more sophisticated science, predict a rise of 2 to 4.5 degrees C—not that far off, considering the relative lack of research in the nineteenth century.[8]

At a 1988 congressional hearing, James Hansen, based on research with his colleagues at the NASA Goddard Institute for Space Studies, had this to say:

> My principal conclusions are: (1) the earth is warmer in 1988 than at any time in the history of instrumental measurements, (2) the global warming is now sufficiently large that we can ascribe with a high degree of confidence a cause and effect relationship to the greenhouse effect, and (3) in our computer climate simulations the greenhouse effect now is already large enough to begin to effect the probability of occurrence of extreme events such as summer heat waves; the model results imply that heat wave/drought occurrences in the Southeast and Midwest United States may be more frequent in the next decade than in climatological (1950–1980) statistics.[9]

More recent research confirms the challenge. According to scientists ranging from China, the USA, Holland, and Great Britain, there is great concern that climate warming will continue to grow to the point of disrupting our global patterns of demographics:

> We demonstrate that depending on scenarios of population growth and warming, over the coming fifty years, one to three billion people are projected to be left outside the climate conditions that have served humanity well over the past 6,000 years.[10]

On the other hand, there are many scientists, 500 in this case, who believe in their hearts that there is nothing at all to worry about. Their conclusion:

> Climate policy relies on inadequate models. Climate models have many shortcomings and are not remotely plausible as policy tools. Moreover, they most likely exaggerate the effect of greenhouse gases such as CO_2.[5]

So, who is responsible for a conspiracy of trust in this case? Which of the alternate realities should we believe?

If we could look at records that go back beyond the eighteenth century, before the history of instrumental measurements, what might we find? Well, how do you find records of our weather before there were instruments to measure them?

The Blossoming of Scarce Data

How about the timing of the blooming of cherry blossoms in Japan? Residents of Kyoto, Japan have been measuring the arrival of spring by the blooming of their cherry blossoms for hundreds of years. These records date back to the year 812, more than 1,200 years ago. In the year 2021, the trees blossomed on March 26. They typically blossom in April. The last time such an early blooming occurred was on March 27 in 1236, 1409, and 1612—not very often. Over the past seventy years, though, the average March temperatures in Kyoto have climbed from 47.5 degrees to 51.1 degrees Fahrenheit, according to data from the Japan Meteorological Agency.[11] That's an increase of two full Celsius degrees in only sixty-eight years—quite troubling by any measure. The most likely cause is climate warming.

For an alternative to finding evidence that goes back hundreds of years, what about getting evidence from scientists ranging across the globe? The Intergovernmental Panel on Climate Change (IPCC) with 270 scientists from sixty-seven different countries has found "increasingly severe, interconnected, and often irreversible impacts of climate change on ecosystems, biodiversity, and human systems; differing impacts across regions, sectors and communities." Their overall conclusion, after all the data analysis from across the globe is daunting:

> The cumulative scientific evidence is unequivocal: climate change is a threat to human well-being and planetary health. Any further delay in concerted anticipatory global action on adaptation and mitigation will miss a brief and rapidly closing window of opportunity to secure a livable and sustainable future for all.[12]

A later report by the same group indicated that we only have to the end of this decade tomove away from fossil fuels and toward clean energy to avoid warming our planet by more than the stated goal of 1.5 degrees Celsius, or 2.7 degrees Fahrenheit.[13]

"Every year that you let pass without going for these urgent emissions reductions makes it more and more difficult," said Jim Skea, an energy researcher at Imperial College London who helped lead the report.[14]

Another study, this one in *Nature Climate Change*, revealed that the Amazon rain forest is reaching a tipping point that may transform it into mere grasslands.[15]

Meanwhile, another record high of annual methane increase was reported by the National Oceanic and Atmospheric Administration, climbing from 1,625 parts per billion in 1980 to 1,900 in 2021. The same report revealed an increase in CO_2 from 340 parts per million in 1980 to 420 in 2021.[16]

The move toward adaptation as opposed to prevention is unmistakable. Even the future of adaptation is now under question. "The science could not be clearer," declared Tina Stege, the Marshall

Islands' climate envoy. "Failure to adapt to this crisis will cost lives."[17] Notice the mention of "adapt" as opposed to "prevent."

For example, several countries in the mid-East were suffering from drought as well as the daunting factors of inflation and scarcity of grains due to the war on Ukraine. One news item reported that countries such as Egypt, Tunisia, Morocco, and Algeria are heavily dependent on grain from Russia and Ukraine, and ongoing inflation requires more adaptation to environmental change than they might be capable of enduring.[18]

According to UN Secretary-General António Guterres,

> We are on a fast track to climate disaster. Major cities under water. Unprecedented heatwaves. Terrifying storms. Widespread water shortages. The extinction of a million species of plants and animals. This is not fiction or exaggeration. It is what science tells us will result from our current energy policies.
>
> We are on a pathway to global warming of more than double the 1.5°C limit agreed in Paris. Some government and business leaders are saying one thing but doing another. Simply put, they are lying. And the results will be catastrophic. This is a climate emergency.
>
> Climate scientists warn that we are already perilously close to tipping points that could lead to cascading and irreversible climate impacts. But, highemitting governments and corporations are not just turning a blind eye, they are adding fuel to the flames.
>
> They are choking our planet, based on their vested interests and historic investments in fossil fuels, when cheaper, renewable solutions provide green jobs, energy security, and greater price stability.[19]

John Kerry, President Biden's special envoy for climate change, stated, "The war in Ukraine and Europe's bid to wean itself from

Russian energy are temporarily disrupting the world's climate progress, but could ultimately accelerate the shift to clean power."[20]

"Every country needs to do more in terms of mitigation, and they need to do more in terms of addressing both adaptation and resilience, no question about it," Kerry said.[21]

This might help to explain our reaction to the sizes of the forest fires across the globe, the frequency of hurricanes,[22,23] the droughts and heat waves accosting farmlands, not to mention the warming of the ocean,[24] even the increase in the probability of future pandemics,[25] and the high costs involved in terms of displacement of millions and related deaths.[26] This is especially dire in light of the fact that only twenty-six of the 193 countries that agreed to limit their contribution to climate warming have done so.[27]

And then there are the corporations that talk a good game in their public statements but don't walk the walk when closer scrutiny reveals what has become known as "greenwashing... when companies make false or exaggerated claims to fool consumers into thinking their products or services benefit the environment."[28] A number of companies, including Shell and KLM, were brought to court to be made accountable for their false claims about sustainability."[29]

But thankfully, there are steps we can take to try and improve the situation,[30,31] and keep the temperature increase over the years down to less than two degrees C[32] even though the scientists at ExxonMobil predicted higher temperature rises over twenty years ago.[33] One approach is to "reforest" the planet, an approach taken by about 175 tree-planting organizations across the globe, planting over 1.4 billion trees across seventy-four countries since 1961.[34, 35] And it may not be as costly as we thought, according to an in-depth accounting of the latest technology for a greener planet. "In response to our opening question, 'Is there a path forward that can get us there cheaply and quickly?', our answer is an emphatic 'Yes!'"[36]

In her book, *The Climate Action Handbook*, Dr. Heidi Roop claims that we can all play a role in saving our planet, both as individuals as well as in more powerful groups. Start with research, she urges, then join communities that work together, and let your passion find expression. "Investing time, energy, and emotion in helping shape the future of your community—say, through being engaged in a community climate action plan or through sharing your own creative talents or advocacy efforts—is critical in a balanced portfolio of climate solutions work."[37]

That's what we'll look at later on.

CHAPTER SIX

The Atlantic Ocean is Running AMOC

> *... there are still those who contend that rapidly reducing the use of fossil fuels would be too painful a price to pay, and that rather than succumb to "alarmism," humanity should learn to "adapt" to a hotter planet.*
>
> —William Falk, editor-in-chief, *THE WEEK*

Imagine donning your scuba gear and taking a deep dive with me into the Atlantic Ocean. In this creatively surreal trip beneath the waves, you can discern two rather large layers of water, one much deeper than the other. The upper layer is the Gulf Stream, known by ocean scientists as the warm, shallow current transferring heat from the tropics to the American Gulf Coast. It then becomes the North Atlantic Drift, as it heads to the British Isles, and then toward the Scandinavian countries and the ice bordering the North Pole. On the other side of the globe, that shallow, warm ocean heads northward to the Indian and Pacific Oceans.

The water, cooled by the northern regions, then becomes heavier and sinks to transform into the lower layer, the cold and saltier deep current, carrying water back toward the tropics. These two levels that you can imagine seeing (and feeling) are collectively referred to as the Great Ocean Conveyor Belt or more technically, the Atlantic Meridional Overturning Circulation (AMOC). It's a dynamic yet reliable belt of flowing ocean that keeps our seasonal temperatures quite stable—at least until recently.

As we dive into the first, higher level, the Gulf Stream, you can feel bathed in its warmth as it flows northward. And, as we continue downward toward the lower level, only about 3,000 to 5,000 meters, it feels saltier and much cooler, now drifting southward. This level is referred to as the North Atlantic Deep Water, which it obviously is. That is the simple version of the AMOC, the effect of which is to distribute heat from the tropics to the northern areas of the globe.

Okay, you can come out of the water now and dry yourself off with some warm towels. What you've just witnessed has been functioning just fine for millennia until quite recently.

Now, the reason I invited you to take this fantasy dive is to introduce you to a real problem that is of great concern to weather scientists. It turns out that the effectiveness of the AMOC was seen to decline starting in the nineteenth century and even more dramatically in the twentieth, weakening about 15 percent since then. What this means, among other consequences, is warmer weather in the Gulf Stream.[1]

More recent research confirms the issue of warming oceans. Several climate scientists from the US, the UK, and Sweden found that a specific site in Antarctica has been measured to be warmer than normal. With very complex scientific instruments and mathematical calculations available to them, the scientists concluded that there were newly emerging conditions "which are comparatively warm, for enhanced heat transport to the ice base," contributing to the faster melting of the Antarctic ice base.[2]

The last time this happened was about 8,200 years ago, causing the Laurentian ice sheet to melt prematurely and flood the Atlantic coastline. We don't want that to happen again. Right now, the AMOC is at its weakest since then. This is because the flow of the AMOC is slower now, resulting in reduced northward flow of heat as well as a shift to the north of the Gulf Stream.

If this continues to deteriorate, which models predict because of the melting of ice off East Greenland, then, according to an article in *Scientific American*, "sea levels could ratchet upward along the

US East Coast, key fisheries could be devastated by spiking water temperatures, and weather patterns over Europe could be altered."

Beyond that, the report continues, "That warming leads to higher sea levels along the coast and raises sea temperatures where economically valuable cold-loving species like cod and lobster live." Using various indicators based on scientific measurements, climate scientists have found that "Excess basal melting in recent decades has increased dynamic mass loss of grounded ice, which has increased Antarctica's contribution to sea-level rise."[3] Other researchers report, "Heat waves smashed temperature records around the globe. Glaciers lost ice at accelerating rates. Sea levels continued to swell."[4]

Baby, It's Hot Out There

In 2021 Death Valley, characteristically very warm, hit a historical high of 130 degrees F. Even the Siberian town of Verkhoyansk, typically one of the coldest places on Earth, hit a high of 100 degrees. Scientists believe this is the consequence of dumping 156 million pounds of toxic gases into the atmosphere every minute of the day.[5]

> That's over nine billion pounds every hour.

In the past administration, there was a strong denial of systemic climate warming. And so, there was no attempt to thwart the oncoming disaster should we not overcome this conspiracy of trust. In the past decade, the hottest in recorded history, there has been over $807 billion in weather-related costs due to the damage inflicted.

What are the causes? It all starts with an increase of CO_2 in our atmosphere, at the rate mentioned above, along with methane and chlorofluorocarbons. This results in the greenhouse effect, which allows more visible radiation from the sun, locking in the heat as the return radiation from Earth's surface is blocked by the greenhouse gases. The result is a clear increase in temperature.

Breaking the Solar Budget

Have you ever heard of the solar budget? This is simply the ratio between the solar radiation entering the Earth and the Earth's ability to reflect the heat back into space. This has been a very constant ratio for eons until around 1900 or thereabouts. Then, with the increased use of coal to fire the plants of the Industrial Revolution and the cutting of forests to make for more farmland to feed more people as they congregated into towns and then larger cities, the noxious gases increased exponentially over the decades.

Very suddenly, at least from the perspective of the life of the Earth, the air became contaminated, and the solar budget was deeply disturbed. The air got warmer, causing dramatic deviations from the weather patterns that had continued undisturbed for centuries and centuries. Over the past ten years, we've experienced more and more disturbingly destructive weather patterns, which have become blatantly undeniable.

In addition to the raging forest fires we see each summer in California and Oregon, the dramatic increase in hurricanes coming through Louisiana, the droughts in our farmlands, there are also similar disasters in Australia, and cyclones in Africa's eastern areas, spawning perfect conditions for unusually large swarms of locusts which devoured all the crops in their paths, causing poverty and starvation among tens of millions of Africans in their path.

The future, unfortunately, bodes even worse, costing the world economy over $23 trillion by 2050, according to the insurance firm, Swiss Re, including "heat waves, wildfires, droughts and torrential rainfall," according to the company's chief economist, Jerome Jean Haegeli, One of the outcomes will be rising rates for flood insurance and this has already begun. According to our government statistics, "In 2020, the US experienced a record-smashing twenty-two weather or climate disasters, including a record seven linked to landfalling hurricanes or tropical storms."[6]

As the World Turns Warmer ... in a Microsecond

All this began with the Industrial Revolution, blossoming into fruition, or more aptly put, building into a crisis, over the past hundred years or so. The primary culprits are use of coal and fossil fuels as sources of energy. A warmer Earth becomes less stable weather-wise, upsetting the usual rhythms and cycles of air currents around the globe. According to the National Oceanic and Atmospheric Administration, the last four years have been the warmest in the past 139 years of recorded history.

According to Samantha Gross, Director of the Energy Security and Climate Initiative, "Many of the impacts that climate models predict in a warming world are happening now, including sea-level rise; stronger cycles of rain and drought; and migration of plants, animals, and people to different areas in reaction to temperature change or resource scarcity."[7]

This instability causes more frequent and intense storms. As well, the warmer temperatures melt ice and snow, which played the part of reflecting the sun's warmth. Now those formerly frozen areas absorb more solar heat, warming the oceans to cause the frequent and intense storms. Also, as the permafrost continues melting, it releases the tons of CO_2 that it had stored for eons and eons, causing even higher temperatures and more melting and more storms, and so on.

In the early spring of 2020, temperatures in the Antarctic reached a high of sixty-nine degrees F, as glaciers continued to melt at dramatic rates.

So where do the CO_2 and other noxious chemicals come from?

Over the past seventy years, as mentioned above, the Atlantic Ocean has been affected in such a way that its current has slowed by about 15 percent, shifting rain patterns, causing colder winters and warmer summers. According to physics professor Lijing Cheng,

The amount of heat we have put into the world's oceans in the past twenty-five years equals 3.6 billion Hiroshima atom bomb explosions . . . The vast majority of global warming heat ends up deposited in the world's oceans, and ocean heat content (OHC) change is one of the best—if not the best—metric for climate change. In 2018, continued record heat was measured in the Earth's climate system. In fact, 2018 has set a new record of ocean heating, surpassing 2017, which was the previous warmest year ever recorded.[8]

All this results in more intense weather disruptions, leading to the fires raging on the West Coast and increases in temperatures as much as 1.8 degrees in California in the past forty years—a scintilla of a microsecond in the life of our planet.

Silver Carp among the Gold(en Law of Unintended Consequences)

According to Elizabeth Kolbert, author of *Under a White Sky*, our attempts to control fish in our waterways as we try to make the best of a challenging situation, seem beyond our ability.[9] Silver carp introduced into an Arkansas pond might end up in the lakes of Illinois.

This has caused quite a kerfuffle among states having to deal with this catastrophe. The waterways connecting Illinois, Mississippi, and Des Plaines Rivers leading to Lake Michigan are replete with the dominant, fish-eating silver carp, menacing the $70 million dollar shipping industry that relies on locks between the various waterways. This is the world's largest freshwater lake system, and the silver carp are destroying the native fish that were the bread and butter of the fishing industry there. So, there is a legal battle to keep these carp out of the Great Lakes.

These Asian carp were initially brought into the Southern aquaculture facilities to clean them out by consuming the algae that accumulated in the tanks, as well as human sewage and swine manure, but they were inadvertently released into nearby ponds. Flooding in the late 1980s and early '90s allowed them to escape from the Southern aquaculture facilities and, voilà, silver carp then, through the variously connected waterways, threatened the Great Lakes. Between 1991 and 1993, the carp multiplied one hundred-fold along the Illinois River upstream of St. Louis. Between 1999 and 2000, the carp multiplied another six hundred-fold downstream of Peoria, Illinois.

What was so scary was that the wild species of the Great Lakes, already on the brink of extinction, would have little chance of surviving this piscine immigration. This could affect not only the $4.6 million annual recreational and commercial fishing industries but also the $2.6 billion annual waterfowl hunting industry and a $12.8 billion travel industry in the Great Lakes areas.

All this resulted in several lawsuits among various states, mostly against Illinois, mostly about closing the locks and keeping the Great Lakes ecologically protected from the terrible carp, with the hope of restoring original conditions. The best solution the courts could come up with involved electric barriers against the carps' migration at strategic points, but also including "a multi-tiered defense encompassing all aspects of monitoring, surveillance, structural solutions, biological controls, and eradication response options."[10]

Now why do I tell you all this, this tale of complex logistic and legal twists and turns? The point of this somewhat convoluted fish story is that most often the best-laid schemes o' mice and men— including high-falutin' attorneys and scientists—go oft awry, to borrow a famous quote from Robert Burns.

> No matter how hard we try and how devoted we may be to save our planet, the path forward is extremely challenging. It took the Earth billions of years to arrive to where it is today and changing one small element in this extremely complex dynamic of earth,

> wind and fire, or the fuels that feed the fire, cannot be easily changed overnight.

But we must keep trying, as not doing anything will certainly lead to catastrophic consequences.

Turning Calm Blue into Popping White

The title of Elizabeth Kolbert's book, *Under a White Sky*, relates to the innovation of controlling the temperature of the atmosphere by spraying sunlight reflecting particles into the air, which replaces the peaceful blue of the sky with a popping-out white—those darn unintended consequences!

According to author Kolbert:

> People have, by now, directly transformed more than half the ice-free land on Earth—some twenty-seven million square miles—and indirectly half of what remains. We have dammed or diverted most of the world's major rivers. Our fertilizer plants and legume crops fix more nitrogen than all terrestrial ecosystems combined, and our planes, cars, and power stations emit about a hundred times more carbon dioxide than volcanoes do. In the age of man, there is nowhere to go, and this includes the deepest trenches of the oceans and the middle of the Antarctic ice sheet, that does not already bear our Friday-like footprints.[9]

Of the largest forest fires, five have been recorded in the past four years. Hundreds of homes were destroyed in Oregon. In Malden, Washington, most of the homes were destroyed. In Okanoga, a one-year-old infant was killed. In mid-September, a total of seven people were found dead. Over 2.5 million acres were burned in California this year.

According to twenty-four climate experts, we may have reached the point of no return. When interviewed by *The New York Times*, their answers were "by turns alarming, cynical and hopeful."[11]

As mentioned above, our glaciers are melting faster and faster, creating another crisis in the climate change disaster.[12] According to an article in *Nature Climate Change*, "Over the past decade, there have been increasing numbers of extreme warm winter air-temperature events linked to decreasing winter sea ice and early season rain-on-snow events with dire ecological consequences." The scientists writing this article end up reporting, "this region is likely to experience extremes in temperature, sea ice, and precipitation phase far outside anything experienced in the past century and probably much longer."[13]

Was there some political account that might help put all this this in historical perspective?

Some History

According to a thorough documentary on Big Oil's power and influence against the truth about climate warming, the awareness of global warming and the need to limit carbon dioxide emissions became noticeable with Al Gore's urging. President George W. Bush initially appeared to be on the side of protecting the planet from pollution during his candidacy but was quickly convinced to yield to Big Oil's concerns about their own commercial prosperity after his inauguration.

Deb Callahan, proponent for a healthy planet, believed that the newly elected President Bush would work against carbon pollution but was saddened by his turn away from that ideal. Bush was swayed by Big Oil's concerns for energy costs and fears of killing the economy. Politically, there was no appetite for addressing global warning.

During the years from 1998 to 2014, Big Oil, primarily Exxon Mobil, did its best to create a sense of uncertainty about the science measuring climate change. Though they claimed sincerity in their statements, they were doing the research and knew as well as any other group of scientists the dire realities of carbon emissions.

During this time, Exxon Mobil and Koch Industries did their best to create an "unsettled science" about the greenhouse effect and were able to displace those scientists who explained the true science of climate change to the public. Lee Raymond and then Rex Tillerson, then consecutive CEOs of Exxon Mobil, promoted so-called advertorials to create uncertainty about climate change. They lobbied to prevent senators on both sides of the aisle to see things their way and prevent legislation that was being considered, and to present climate change as a hoax.

At one point, Nancy Pelosi and Newt Gingrich presented themselves as united for such legislation but to no avail. As well, President Obama and Senator McCain joined hands across the aisle for the legislation. But Exxon Mobil's funding against it was too much to deal with.

Al Gore, with his book, *An Inconvenient Truth,* fought back valiantly, but with little effect, except for those who were already committed to the cause.

When Rex Tillerson was open enough to see the way to a constructive position to stopping the effect of fossil fuels on the atmosphere, there was enough momentum to pass the climate change bill by a vote of 219 to 212 in the summer of 2009.[14]

That year, the Tea Party, funded in part by the Koch brothers, became a force to be reckoned with. The progressive left lost out as protesters against cutting carbon emissions began to show their power, while the Koch brothers continued to fund conservative candidates for government. The issues of rising energy costs and hurting the coal industry proved daunting.[15]

More recently, just prior to the arrival of COVID-19, as energy stocks became less profitable, climate change became more of an issue, but by 2022 they had regained their value. So now there are at least two forces to reckon with: a successful energy industry and the call for a healthier planet.

Oil companies have known about the harmful consequences of their profit-oriented practices for decades. Yet they silenced their own scientists so their profits wouldn't be affected. When Shell CEO Ben van Beurden was asked about this, he replied, "Yeah, we knew. Everybody knew."[16] He went on to explain that a corporation's role is to make a profit, that Shell was doing what it was designed to do, and that it was up to other institutions in our society to take on the concerns of saving the planet from climate disaster.

Even President Biden, in the spring of 2023, initiated an $8 billion oil drilling project in the pristine wilderness at the North Slope of Alaska, succumbing to intense pressure by oil executives despite his campaign promises to avoid doing this kind of exploitation.[17]

Then there are the politics of poor nations trying to survive the challenges of a difficult global economy. The Democratic Republic of Congo, where large rain forests store an abundance of carbon, has decided to auction off its lands for oil investments. This is in total opposition to what the planet needs. According to Irene Wabiwa, who oversees the Congo Basin Forest, "If oil exploitation takes place in these areas, we must expect a global climate catastrophe, and we will just have to watch helplessly."[18]

All this is causing the catastrophe to affect where people can manage to live. In the US, climate change is making migration an issue. In California wine country, fires are leaving neighborhoods abandoned. In Texas, floods in low-lying areas seem continuous. According to Jake Bittle, author of *The Great Displacement*,

> by the end of the century, twenty million Americans will be displaced because of climate issues, and politicians seem to be looking the other way.

"The planet is well past caring whether pandering politicians want to play ball," he writes. "The alarm bells are ringing. We need to wake up."[19]

We have a bit of time left to save the planet, but not much. According to the IPCC, the critical threshold will occur within the coming decade. This report, agreed upon by 195 nations, maintains that, over the next ten years, if nothing is done to control it, temperatures are predicted to rise 2.7 degrees F. above preindustrial levels. It "is quite clear that whatever future we end up with is within our control," according to Piers Foster, a climate scientist at the University of Leeds. "It is up to humanity to determine what we end up with."[20]

When people start dying of heat at a sports event, then we know how serious these reports are. At an open-air Indian government event in the outskirts of Mumbai on a Sunday afternoon, the temperature reached 100.4 degrees F. Baking in the hot sun, elven individuals passed away and over fifty were hospitalized, according to Maharashtra's chief minister, Eknath Shinde.[21] According to the Indian government, the top temperatures were at least three degrees C. higher than normal.[22]

"Climate records have shown us that the window to act is closing," reports Simonetta Cheli, Director of Earth Observation Programs. "Melting glaciers, recent droughts and floods in Europe, as well as more extreme weather events," she adds, "are telling us that it's time to act now."[23]

And so, the war against air pollution was overwhelmed by money and politics from the beginning . . . and continues.

CHAPTER SEVEN

What, Me Worry?

It is immoral for oil and gas companies to be making record profits from this energy crisis on the backs of the poorest people and communities, at a massive cost to the climate.

—UN Secretary-General António Guterres on Aug. 3, 2022

Some say it's almost too late. Across the country we see unusual rainfall, snowfall, storms, flooding, tornadoes, and the resultant decimation of species, particularly as drought and wildfires ravage the West.[1] We hear about the resistance to participation in global initiatives to battle climate change by China and India.[2] Other obstacles exist as well.

Yet there is hope if we do act quickly and decisively. In April 2021, the Biden administration introduced a $2 trillion plan to focus on a number of items including $174 billion for electric vehicle incentives, $100 billion for electric grid and clean energy, $46 billion for clean energy manufacturing, and $35 billion for climate technology.[3] In addition, $115 billion, slated for improved roads and bridges, would, according to the *Times*, have a climate angle: the new roads and bridges would be built to withstand the high waters and brutal storms of a changing climate."[4]

Biden hoped to cut emissions in half as he addressed a meeting of forty nations. Some agreed, but others, like Russia, India, and China, gave no promises.[5]

With all this good government intention to make our world a safer place, there are still highly trained scientists who question whether climate change is real. As Steven Koonin, former undersecretary for science in the Obama administration's Department of Energy, writes in his book, *Unsettled*, "both the research literature and government reports that summarize and assess the state of climate science say clearly that . . . the warmest temperatures in the US have not risen in the past fifty years."

As part of a team of six leading climate experts and six leading physicists meeting together after two months of study to give an opinion on the state of what was known about climate change, Koonin concluded that climate models disagree with, or even contradict, each other, and that government and UN press releases and summaries do not accurately reflect the reports themselves. He does admit that humans exert a growing, but physically small, warming influence on the climate. "In short," he concludes, "the science is insufficient to make useful projections about how the climate will change."

His research into the literature of the most recent reports by the US government and the UN led him to surmise that humans have had no detectable impact on hurricanes over the past century and that Greenland's ice sheet isn't shrinking any more rapidly today than it was eighty years ago. His conclusion? "The net economic impact of human-induced climate change will be minimal through at least the end of this century."[6]

This lack of consensus, even among highly trained scientists, is concerning.

What we find in the streets of our towns and cities is quite troublesome as well, but not because of "unsettled" data, but rather because of our direct experiences. "Wildfires are bigger and starting earlier in the year. Heat waves are more frequent. Seas are warmer, and flooding is more common. The air is getting hotter. Even ragweed pollen season is beginning sooner" writes Christopher Flavelle of *The New York Times*. "There is no small town, big city, or rural community that is unaffected by the climate crisis," Michael S. Regan, the Environmental

Protection Agency (EPA) administrator, said. "Americans are seeing and feeling the impacts up close, with increasing regularity."[7]

The Haunting Prospect of International Cooperation

The only way to avoid burning up our planet with irreversible temperature increase is, as we hear over and over, to act immediately, not in two years or ten years, as so many plans offer. The International Energy Agency (IEA), made up of most of the countries in the world, with its research backed by the International Monetary Fund, maintains that reaching our goals to save the planet would involve "vast amounts of investment, innovation, skillful policy design and implementation, technology deployment, infrastructure building, international cooperation, and efforts across many other areas."

With over thirty-six international authors and more than sixty peer reviewers, this is quite a substantial piece of research. The challenge, according to this 222-page report, is for all countries to quickly shift from fossil fuels to sustainable forms of energy such as wind and solar. This incredibly thorough report, ultimately, has no secret weapon to achieve the desired results, even after all the data have been churned and graphically displayed.

The most revealing note in this carefully written report with so many sources is the following remark on Page 189, that "depending on international cooperation slows the deployment of mitigation options that are currently in the demonstration phase." A graph clearly depicts how such "weak international cooperation" would affect the end result of all this planning.

Instead of reaching the stated goal by 2030, such "weak cooperation," the more likely outcome, as one might expect, based on past and current experience, would result in reaching the goal by close to 2090. In other words, the best-laid plans of men and climate scientists "go oft awry," to quote Burns once again. The many authors of this well-meaning report admit as much. "A strong push is needed for the demonstration of key technologies, especially for complex technologies in emerging markets and developing economies."

Who will provide this "strong push" and how will it be enforced? The point here is that the theory of preventing climate change, even by the most informed and well-funded scientists, sounds too much like a pipe dream. We are in this mess much deeper than we realize. "Without international cooperation, emissions will not fall to net zero by 2050," the authors agree.[8]

A look at any current political talks about preventing climate warming reveals the terrible truth as to how difficult it is to get such international cooperation so necessary. Recall how even a nation as powerful and rich as the US dropped out of the Paris Agreement when we had a president who did not see the big picture. How can smaller countries across the globe be counted on to cooperate with all the diversity in attitude toward climate change?

"The sheer magnitude of changes needed to get to net-zero emissions by 2050 is still not fully understood by many governments and investors," Fatih Birol, the agency's executive director, said in an interview.[9]

Cyril Widdershoven, a longtime observer of the international energy market, concludes that "the approach suggested by the IEA is not only impossible but also reckless."[10]

Conspiracy May Be the Easier Answer, After All Is Said and Done

> It appears that we, as a culture, are like the proverbial frog in a pan of water, slowly heating up as we sit, not able to acknowledge the rising temperature that may soon boil us alive.

But sometimes it is hard to ignore the increasing temperature even for a frog sitting in the pan.

In mid-summer of 2021, the temperature in the Southwest was reaching a boiling point—128 degrees F in Lake Havasu City, Arizona[11] with temperatures in downtown Los Angeles reaching 100 degrees F while the prolonged drought continued.[12] Seattle, with cool, rainy days as its signature, reached an astounding 108 degrees, passing the record June high of 96.[13] Canada, which we often visualize with snow on the ground, reached temperatures of 116 degrees on its West Coast.[14]

Over a billion marine animals, including mussels, clams, hermit crabs, tiny sea cucumbers, and sea stars, were dying in the Pacific Northwest. "It just feels like one of those postapocalyptic movies," said Christopher Harley, a marine biologist at the University of British Columbia who studies the effects of climate change on coastal marine ecosystems.[15] All this because of climate change, according to Geert Jan van Oldenborgh of the Royal Netherlands Meteorological Institute.[16]

It's even gotten to the point where it might make more sense to sell the water needed to grow produce than to grow the produce.[17] One-third of our food production, according to scientists calling for "interlinked climate change mitigation,"[18] may be affected by this trend in rising temperature.

Climate change is killing humans as well. According to earth scientists, the Earth is now 1 to 2 degrees Celsius higher than ever, with the highest temperatures in Guatemala, Paraguay, Kuwait, and Iran. And it's killing people all over the planet, with 37 percent of heat-related deaths due to man-made climate change, according to seventy earth scientists working in concert across the globe.[19] It's also drowning people, as happened when heavy rains caused overflowing in Belgium and Germany in mid-summer 2021. Hundreds were unaccounted for due to the rain's destruction.[20] Climate change, according to scientists who study this, costs the country over $820 billion a year in terms of healthcare,[21] and is sufficiently destructive to cause wildfires to rage over one million acres across the western United States and Canada.[22]

In India over the past ten years, long dry spells are being followed by more frequent and more intense short-term rainfalls during the monsoon season, causing destructive flooding. Temperature has increased by 0.7 degrees C, resulting in "cyclones of greater intensity . . . Increasing extreme rainfall events and droughts are both, ironically, detrimental to groundwater recharge," according to the scientists doing the measurements.[23] Sea levels have risen three centimeters, leading to a loss of about sixty-five feet along the coastline.

Based on all this, some say it's too late to deal with climate change. The effects of it are already making us suffer, as we've just seen. What we really need to deal with is the adjustment to what's already happening. According to Juan Moreno-Cruz of the University of Waterloo, "The impacts of climate change are here. Let's talk about climate realism . . . We need to provide adaptation measures and investments to the majority of people on the planet."[24]

The bad news, according to a report approved of by 195 governments and based on over 140,000 studies,[25] is that we are already on an irreversible path to higher temperatures and the consequences that come with it, such as record-breaking heat that we saw in the Pacific Northwest and southern Europe; more frequent flooding as we saw in China, India, and Germany; greater likelihood of droughts, followed by torrents of rain, as we saw in the western states; and rising sea levels that might threaten coastal cities like Miami, all signs of what some are calling "Code Red for Humanity."[26]

> The good news is that there is still some room for adjustment as we enter the adaptation phase.

According to the IPCC, if we can replace fossil fuels with other resources and stop cutting down forests, we can still manage to keep the climate from warming up too much.

But we're quickly running out of time. According to Malik Amin Aslam, a climate change government officer reporting to the prime minister of Pakistan, "What science is now saying is actually happening in front of our eyes. It's like a hammer hitting us on the head every day."[27]

And that hammer continues to hit us even harder as time goes on. Based on current data, scientists predict that the probabilities of weather extremes are going to increase by at least 100 percent at best and 700 percent at worst over the next thirty years.[28]

I have offered you the truths I've gleaned after looking at the scientific literature as well as the comments of some of the deniers who call this issue a big hoax. Now I leave you with the greatest responsibility of all: to take personal action or accept the inevitable. It is very tempting to accept the alternate reality that all will be well when the day is done—extremely tempting. And we can justify that option with the information that supports it. Information and "scientific" opinion to bolster up that alternate reality are very available in this Age of Disinformation.

> But there are things we can do.

When shopping for food, we can be aware that there are some companies that respect our planet and produce food accordingly. White Oak Pastures, in South Georgia, for example, describes in detail how they produce food while taking into consideration the need for sustainability.

Their three core values involve animal welfare, land regeneration, and rural revival.

1) **Animal welfare** includes open pastures and a zero-waste model, "turning unused products like hides and tallow into handmade consumer goods and composting all inedible viscera to return

nutrients to the soil in our pastures." All foods fed to the animals are non-GMO products.

2) **Land regeneration** involves mitigating climate change, "confirmed that our farm is storing more carbon in our soil than our pasture-raised cows emit during their lifetime."[29]

3) Located in small-town Bluffton, a poverty-based community of 103 people, the company pays their 155 employees more than twice the county average and have reversed a ten-year decline in the town's economy. Workshops offered throughout the year include such topics as **soil health management, humane animal handling, and organic vegetable gardening**.

In addition to selecting such sustainable enterprises, each of us can take personal responsibility to reduce the negative effect that cattle have on our environment. The methane of hundreds of millions of farm animals creates up to 15 percent of all greenhouse gases, not to mention the deforestation required to provide land on which to cultivate them, and the feed and water they consume. So here are some ways to take responsibility and reduce this problem:

- Reduce the serving size of the red meat portions you eat daily, possibly to three ounces, the size of a pack of playing cards.
- Swap out your meat portions by choosing a chicken or fish sandwich instead of a burger.
- Experiment with plant-based "burger" alternatives till you find one that really satisfies you.[30]

> At the end of the day, there is always hope.

Bill Gates maintains that innovation will save the day. He's very smart, and very resourceful. Let's hope he's right. Even previously denying Republicans have begun to turn around and admit that climate change is not a hoax after all.[31] Maybe they were influenced by Greta Thunberg, who put it: "We are in a crisis of crises. A pollution crisis. A climate crisis. A children's rights crisis. We will not allow the world to look away."[32]

There is no doubt about the crisis. Economics, not surprisingly, seems to take priority over planetary welfare.[33] The news keeps revealing how climate change is taking second place to economics in virtually all western governments, remaining totally out of sync with the Paris Agreement limits.[34]

By the summer of 2022, there were reports of over 2,000 people dying due extreme heat in Portugal and Spain, and the longest river in Italy, the Po River, was running dry, threatening the year's harvest, while political leaders chose the priority of political economics over long-term concerns for your planet's destiny.[35]

The net result? If we don't act quickly, the consequences can be dire. According to top medical journals like *Lancet*, "climate change is set to become the 'defining narrative of human health,' ... triggering food shortages, deadly disasters, and disease outbreaks that would dwarf the toll of the coronavirus."[36]

In the record hot summer of 2022, as the planet sweltered in unprecedented temperatures,[37, 38] US Senator Joe Manchin withdrew his support for climate change measures in favor of short-term profits.[39]

Russia's invasion of Ukraine has not helped either, causing many European countries to fall back on reliance on fossil fuels.[40] Then there's the Supreme Court ruling against the climate-saving regulations of the Environmental Protection Agency.[41]

And yet there is plenty of good news as well. As author and journalist Charles C. Mann reveals:

Food production has outpaced population growth in the last fifty years; we're living longer, with average life expectancy going from 53.6 in 1960 to 72.4 in 2017; there are many fewer deaths due to childbirth, half the number since 1990; there is greater access to drinking water globally, from 80.6 percent in 1990 to 89.8 percent in 2015; and more people around the world have access to electricity, from 76.7 percent in 1993 to 88.9 percent in 2017.[42]

Also, there is hope in the progress of green technology: Growing research in airplanes that are powered by batteries rather than fossil fuels which contribute significantly to air pollution. Also, there is very hopeful research on tapping ocean tides for green energy.

The European Marine Energy Centre, off the coast of Scotland, has founded a company, Orbital Marine, which has developed the O2, a 680-ton body resembling a fuselage with two ten-meter-long underwater turbines continuously being pushed to turn at a rate of twelve revolutions/minute, generating 2,000 megawatts. The Israeli startup, Eco Wave Power, now has projects that affix wave-driven generators to onshore features like breakwaters, with projects in Gibraltar, Portugal, and the Port of Los Angeles.[43]

Finally, there was the legislation signed in August 2022 that put into law several climate change initiatives[44] that other countries can follow.[45] The bill allocated $369 billion to reduce carbon emissions by 40 percent in 2030.[46]

As Jeff Bezos proclaimed on getting back to Earth after his landmark flight from space on July 20th of 2021 and asked what was most memorable about seeing the planet from the boundary of space, he replied,

> "It's one planet, and we share it, and it's fragile."

Actor William Shatner, who was also on Jeff Bezos' space shuttle, was sad upon returning to Earth. "I was in grief for the Earth," as he descended from the rocket, he told the press. "I am aware that every moment that goes by, things that took five billion years to emerge are going extinct . . . I discovered that the beauty isn't out there. It's down here, with all of us."

RADICAL STRATEGIES: OUR RESPONSE TO CLIMATE CHANGE

So How Can We Be Trusted by Our Children to Make a Difference in Their Futures?

There are diametrically opposing views as to whom to trust about climate change. Some continue to characterize it as a hoax, while others respect the scientific viewpoint with all its statistical observations. Then there are those who experience the effects firsthand, such as the inhabitants where forest fires have done unforeseen damage, where flooding has caused the loss of homes, where hurricanes increase in frequency way beyond historical norms. Here are some ways of dealing with this crisis by controlling the change, even if you're still deciding about its long-term effects.

Systemic

Every creature in our environment has its own niche of importance. We may not know all the science of it but there's a comprehensive dynamic that makes it all work, from corals and plankton to the largest of whales. It's called our ecosystem in which organisms feed off one another, trees breathe the CO_2 we exhale, and bird poop distributes plant seeds in excellent fashion. That's how we maintain a supply of fresh fish, have our air freshened, and obtain the fruits and grains we eat, all natural. Even the shark's presence, in some locales, keeps turtles from overgrazing vegetation at the bottom of the water.

> It is our responsibility to do what we can to keep this ecology working for our very existence, as well as for the pleasure of observing and enjoying nature.

As humans, we can do our part, as outlined in the following points.

1) Preventing habitat loss and overexploitation: Deforestation and overfishing are some of the main culprits of habitat loss, along with man-made pollution. We can, if we choose, reforest certain areas long shorn of their original trees. Healthy forests are essential for the air we breathe and for controlling carbon in our atmosphere. Unfortunately, countries like Brazil are cutting their forests with impunity at an increasing rate. Political pressure is one way to combat this terrible destruction of trees.

2) Government regulation: why do we need an Environmental Protection Agency? Because our day-to-day activities involve the consumption of natural resources as well as air and water. We need governmental oversight to tend to environmental concerns that affect us all. We can reconstitute the integrity of the EPA with its emphasis on protection, just as its name clearly declares.

3) Tax credits for research and development of renewable energy and carbon capture and storage projects: We can continue the attempt to reduce greenhouse gases through research and implement potential solutions such as capturing CO_2 emitted from power plants and storing it via afforestation or in the ocean. The Paris Agreement, initiated in November 2016, was signed by almost all nations, 195 of them committed to limiting climate change. The Trump administration resigned but President Biden had the US rejoin. The hope is to reach net-zero carbon emission by 2050.

4) Incentivize carbon reduction with tax or cap-and-trade systems: Cap-and-trade, not as simple as carbon tax, involves increasing the cost of emission set by the emissions trading market. Here's how it works. In the US, each company would have a certain *right to pollute.* Any given industrial business is assigned a cap on the amount of CO_2 and other greenhouse gases it can emit into the atmosphere, termed an *emissions cap.* If it comes close to exceeding its assigned amount, it can then purchase the unused amount of another business' allotment if that second company is not using up its assigned limit.

5) More government funds for R&D for innovative research to energize new technology such as the Green New Deal, to discourage use of fossil fuels, and encourage zero-emission resources through solar and wind energy. The primary aim here is to keep the increase in temperature capped at 1.5 degrees C. for the coming years. Beyond that, sea level would be expected to rise from about ten to thirty inches, creating havoc at all coastal residential sites. As well, higher temperatures would result in greater evaporation rates, causing more moisture in the air, more rainfall and resulting flooding. The hope is to establish an economy allowing for clean air and water as well as healthy food in a sustainable environment. So far, at the time of this writing, the Senate has refused to pass such a bill.

6) Continued explorations of energy production such as ITER: thirty-five countries are participating in the International Thermonuclear Experimental Reactor project, located in Southern France, using magnetic confinement plasma physics—nuclear fusion creating hot plasma—slated for use some time in 2100. It will provide a million times more energy than burning coal, three times as much energy as U-235 fission. The two main challenges are to get the raw material hot enough for the process (fifteen million degrees C.) and then building structures to confine the intense hear necessary for this process.

7) Bill Gates' TerraPower—mini-fission reactors, known as small modular reactors, or SMRs. Link up twelve together and it can power a medium-sized city. Gates has invested over $250 million toward the success of this project. One of the main innovations of this $4 billion project is the use of liquid sodium as the coolant rather than water.

8) Underwater farming—using no soil and requiring no pesticides. The farming is done vertically, taking up little space, only one-fifth of normal agricultural practices above ground. This new blue-green economy brings restorative ocean farming of healthier foods without affecting fish supply.

9) The Biden administration is looking to spend billions on clean energy research and development and create over a million jobs in the emerging electric vehicle industry, creating an entirely new energy economy.

Community

10) Aggregation effect through social norms. As each of us does our work to foster a healthier climate, a new norm develops with mutual support and the total of our efforts begins to add up. Individuals join collectives to form communities that choose to take joint action.

11) Educating yourself from reliable scientific sources and speaking up: Let others know your values about climate change. Only this way will our mutual efforts combine to create an emerging community sensible to the need to save our planet for future generations as well as our own. Speaking up can also affect helpful legislation at all levels, including county laws and community regulations for recycling. Community-based programs and summer camps for students start our younger citizens on the right path.

Individual: Grass Roots Level

12) Learning how to power homes with renewable energy, using rooftop solar panels, solar ovens, and Tesla power walls. In some Mediterranean countries, rooftop solar panels have been providing hot water for over fifty years. Only about 8.2 percent of our country is currently getting energy from solar and wind resources despite hopes of getting rid of fossil fuels by 2050. Solar generation of electricity is projected to climb to 48 percent by 2050, making it the fastest-growing electricity source. Wind turbine production of electricity is projected to climb from 7 percent of total US renewable generation in 2017 to 35 percent by 2050.

13) Nuclear power plants have generated about 17 percent of US electricity since 1990. It is projected to remain at 17 percent through 2050.

Until and unless some of the innovations listed above (especially numbers 6 and 7) come to pass, then we, as consumers, are left to do the best we can with what we currently have. Even if we choose to build solar power on our own properties, for example, some states, especially California, make it difficult. It appears that state-affiliated utility companies report being justified in charging fees for solar panel users to pay for the cost of infrastructure for energy delivery to privately owned dwellings, but this may be changing. Political pressure is necessary to continue this shift in philosophy.

Oil-producing countries such as Saudi Arabia are working toward new industries, accepting the fact that we are moving away from fossil fuels in the future. By then, private autos may be a thing of the past as driverless electric vehicles run by private companies can pick us up within minutes and deliver us to our destination safely and easily.

14) **Weatherizing**—reducing utility bills, taking advantage of free home-energy audits, reducing air leakage, bringing insulation up to date, and ensuring good ventilation and moisture control. This is something many of us have been doing for ages. Use energy-efficient appliances by seeking out the Energy Star labels.

15) **Reducing water waste**—lowering your water bill by taking shorter showers, only running full loads of laundry, checking for leaks in toilets and other supply lines. This is also something some have been doing for ages. This is the time to remind all of us.

16) **Eat less meat**. Raising beef and lamb takes up lots of land that could have trees and consumes great quantities of water. The livestock then pollute our air with methane coming from their digestive process. Start slowly by reducing number of meat meals by about 25 percent, then, a couple months later, by 50 percent, eventually only once a week and, finally, about once a month, if at all.

17) **LED lightbulbs**—save $125 over the lifetime of a single bulb. Energy consumption is reduced by 70 percent to 90 percent. In California, incandescent bulbs are no longer available.

18) **Maintain your car**—properly-inflated tires, proper alignment, air filter. Your vehicle is then not only more climate friendly but safer for you as well. Encourage your dealers and repair shops to create inexpensive flyers encouraging this in the context of climate change, helping to improve their image as contributing to the community—a win-win proposition.

19) **Fuel-efficiency** in your vehicles can be achieved simply by driving at slower speeds and braking gently. Consider going electric in your next purchase.

20) **Impact of flying:** Remember, flying accounts for 2.5 percent of global CO_2 emission, or over two-hundred million tons of CO_2 per year.

SECTION IV:

VAXXED

SURVIVING PANDEMICS

CHAPTER EIGHT

Trust in the Age of COVID

The air ... You just breathe the air and that's how it's passed ... This is deadly stuff.

—Donald J. Trump, as told to Bob Woodward

It was all about the stock market not coming down ... It's almost criminal.

—Joe Biden

The way to control our economy is to control the pandemic.

—Tom Frieden, MD, former head of the CDC

On Thanksgiving Day, 2021, we got a very unwelcome surprise. Initially called B.1.1.529, then Omicron, it was a highly unexpected variant, with a very unusual constellation of mutations, and the fear was that it might be more significantly contagious than the Delta variation. I was with some of my family members, some of whom were adamant that vaccines were to be avoided at all costs. The wife of one of my family members declared she'd rather quit her medically oriented job than be forced to take the vaccine. Then, in early 2022, came another variant of Omicron, BA.2, even more contagious.

Two realities. One outcome. That's what it looked like from an objective perspective. Public health officials argued for the guidelines that prevented, as much as possible, contagion of COVID-19 while then-President Trump and his administration had argued for opening the economy when COVID-19 first hist us as a nation. Between the two realities was a wide gulf of mistrust. Ever wonder which side won? Well, here's how it played out.

No Trust Between the Two "Worlds" of COVID-19

Toward the end of March 2020, President Trump was certain that the COVID-19 virus was on its way out and that we'd soon be back to normal. He referred to himself as a "wartime president," waging the war against the insidious virus, of course, and blaming the outbreak on the Chinese by accusing them of not being transparent early on. But the feedback from the long-established US task force could not be summarily dismissed. The US had a team visiting China every year to identify emerging viruses from the wet market, but Trump had dismantled it.

In April of 2020, the White House chief of staff, Mark Meadows, had his office full at eight every morning. Convinced that the COVID-19 pandemic was tapering off and coming to its inevitable end, the White House group was busy promoting a "state authority handoff," shifting responsibility from federal to state officials.

> There was a growing tension between two different worlds—one being public health and the other being commerce.

The first focused on the need for the three Ws: *wear* a mask, *wash* your hands, and *watch* that distance of six feet. The second looked for economic relief from sheltering at home, which kept many people from work and their income so necessary to keep the economy alive.

President Trump and his team were clearly focused on promoting the second world. They were hoping the pandemic was shutting down and thinking that the economy was priority, especially if Trump was to get good numbers by the November election. The pandemic data were being downplayed.

The Bridge

On April 10, Trump, proclaiming his role as a "wartime president," predicted that the number of deaths, because of his excellent leadership, would not go beyond 100,000, and this much only because the Chinese had not been more transparent from the beginning.

On April 11, Dr. Deborah Birx felt comfortable enough with her selected charts to assure the task force that, although Boston and Chicago had not yet reached their peaks, the overall projections by the models looked good and that a flattening of the curve could be anticipated.

After another week of this tension, Trump and his team began to buckle down on pushing their agenda even harder. The economy was not getting any better and the polls began to show a shift against the president.

Dr. Birx, loyal as she could be to the administration while not sacrificing her scientific integrity, offered that the pandemic numbers could be coming down even if there were an opening of the economy, so long as people kept up with the mask-wearing and distancing. It appeared she and her valiant team were trying to create a workable bridge between the two "alternate realities." Dr. Fauci, on the other hand, still had his feet firmly planted with public health, and this divide within the administration continued over time. Dr. Birx had a new set of standards for mitigating the pandemic that she presented to the president, guiding the path over the bridge from one "world" to the other. Trump announced this document to the nation on April 16.

The Model That Just Wouldn't Work

Dr. Birx was depending largely on the Chris Murray Model offered by the University of Washington that predicted state-by-state impacts of the pandemic, but some considered this to be undependable, not taking sufficiently into account the reality that people were not adhering to the public health guidelines, in part due to Trump's influence. Community spread of the disease was wreaking havoc with the anticipated numbers.

When the pandemic turned unexpectedly to higher numbers, Trump was dismayed yet persevered in pushing his agenda. He continued his focus on shifting the responsibility from his desk to those of the state governors. It turned out that so many citizens were confused by the mixed messages emanating from the two different "worlds" that ignoring the three Ws became the option of choice for those whose batteries for sheltering were wearing down.

To bolster his "reality," Trump veered away from the truth and doubled down on his own political needs, ignoring public health factors. He then began to muzzle Dr. Anthony Fauci, chief exponent of the public health world, making his public appearances rare. (When asked by a reporter where Dr. Fauci was at one of the meetings, Trump replied that Dr. Fauci had other things to do that day.) Trump and his team chose to drown the public health figures and push their own view that commerce was the right choice for the nation.

Dr. Birx was in a very challenging position. She hadn't factored in the influence that the Trump team had on encouraging people to ignore the public health guidelines. Then Trump began downplaying the significance of testing, saying at times that testing just revealed more cases of the virus, so why not slow down the testing. He also downplayed the importance of wearing a mask, seeing it as a sign of weakness, as he implied when asked about that issue by a reporter at a White House briefing, accusing her of being too politically correct. Trump kept Dr. Birx on a short leash, even allowing Dr. Atlas, a freewheeling physician who supported Trump's off-base medical opinions, to take central stage, displacing Dr. Birx's influence. All these mixed messages wore away at trust even more.

Tough Decisions

When cornered by the press about his lack of leadership, the president responded that he was doing an excellent job, sharing that he had issued travel restrictions with China. He offered financial support to those absent from work, and help to get Americans more ventilators, personal protective equipment supplies; and encouraging vaccine projects. These were all true, though not without complications for each of them.

Mark Meadows looked at the numbers measuring road traffic and business transactions in order to help make the right decision about opening the economy. It was not an easy decision to make.

By now, the administration could take pride in the fact that the nation could count three million tests processed. But some public health officials reminded the administration that many more were needed—500,000 tests a day, according to Dr. Ashish Jha of the Harvard Global Health Institute. The administration was happy to let the states take on this responsibility.[1]

The task force had been meeting daily with President Trump, but this was to end by April 24. Now Dr. Fauci was being pushed to the sidelines lest he contradict the president's push to open the economy despite the discouraging pandemic figures. By early May, there were considerations for the task force to end its daily meetings as well.

The Bridge Crumbles

Mid-May became even more confusing and frustrating as the flattening that was hoped for was not being manifested. Dr. Birx tried even harder to match the numbers with the administration's hopes for a quick opening up. The bridge between the two alternate realities was beginning to crumble. There was hope against hope that any resurgence would not happen till late fall. Governor Cuomo's leadership in the Northeast including New York, New Jersey, and Connecticut was a shining beacon of success that lit up Birx's hopes. States like Alabama, Texas, and Arizona were eager to move ahead with opening. And, encouraged by Trump, more and more people, particularly in the eager states, were abandoning the three Ws recommended by public health officials like Dr. Fauci, now no longer in the public eye as much.

President Trump was still insisting that testing was widely available at this point when it really was not. Governors who asked for federal help were treated like second-class citizens. Trump was partial to those who would pay special attention to him by calling him personally and asking for a favor. This is what California Governor Gavin Newsom had to do. Several governors started conferring with one another over late-night phone calls to discuss moving ahead with public health guidelines despite Trump's single-minded approach to opening up the economy.

By the beginning of June, it became clear that community spread was creating dramatic increases in infection rates. Was it a Memorial Day celebration? The protests over the George Floyd incident? Or was it a more enduring phenomenon? Like the batteries for sheltering just wearing out, and the need to just get out of the house and let off steam?

By mid-July it was clear to everyone that the bridge that Dr. Birx had worked so hard on preparing would not work. It was not temporary events that were propelling the data. It was a portion of the population just running out of sheltering steam and declaring they had had enough social deprivation, influenced, in part, by Trump's encouragement to "Liberate."

At this point, over five million Americans were infected—an average of over 65,000 new cases a day—with over 150,000 deaths.

Even then, the White House was looking to reduce spending for further testing.

No Trust Lost

Why more in the South than elsewhere? Contributing factors might have been region-specific, like church activities in the southeastern states, the festive culture of New Orleans and surroundings, the tight family gatherings of the Latinos in southern Texas, the beach mentality on the California coast. Beyond these regional cultural factors was the need for people to connect with one another. Given permission by their president, it was easier to let go and declare victory over federal mandates and just go back to enjoying life once more.

As well, it became a political issue. Some were skeptical of the mandate for masks, suspecting that this was one step of government control just leading to more. Shifting mandates, from discouraging masks initially to their high priority later affected many people's trust in both the Food and Drug Administration (FDA) and even the World Health Organization. Indeed, the term *infodemic on coronavirus* came to include all the disinformation websites and blogs encouraging distrust of public health recommendations.[2] Some psychologists saw their patients as "acting out of misinformation . . . for many reasons, including a reliance on noncredible sources, or a perception that some have overemphasized the dangers primarily to discredit President Trump." They concluded, "nobody likes to be told that what they believe is wrong."[3]

Another issue of trust relates to a possible vaccination for the virus. According to reports, many are reluctant to trust a new vaccination, whenever it might appear. A retired teacher from Fairbanks, Alaska was quoted by *The New York Times* as saying, "The bottom line is, I have absolutely no faith in the FDA and in the Trump administration."[4] Mythologies began building about the vaccine leading to the possibility of more easily tracking of the citizenry.

Then the issue of sending children back to school: again, two consensual opinions, mirroring the mask issue. Trump advocated a determined return to schools regardless of the consequences and those cautious about contagion and the probability of raising the curve by bringing the bug back home to families were opposed to a return to the classroom. With a mixed approach between the two, there were pervasive issues of increased contagion in almost every school setting. Even the mask issue was not clear, giving students the option to go either way in many circumstances.

At a North Georgia university, according to news reports, a large private party was held on a Saturday night with most not wearing masks. As for younger children, the American Academy of Pediatrics encouraged sending children back to school, so long as the three Ws were being respected. The theory and aspirations were obvious, but the practicalities did not go well when the mixed messages from the government were considered.

Even teachers were scared to go back to work, given the conflicting guidance. They would wear their masks but many of the schools did not mandate that for the students. So, a growing number of teachers chose not to return, often announcing their decisions on Instagram and Remind, sites popular with teachers.

Yet, in Denmark, the return to school was successful. With a uniform approach by the local municipalities of the Danish government based on a trusting relationship with the teachers' union and parent groups, very few incidents of contagion occurred. What was the formula that worked so well while most American attempts failed? Within a context of respectful trust among the government, teachers' unions, and parent groups, and the clear mandate for mask-wearing, the formula included the decision to put groups of twenty-five children in "bubbles" that involved consistent social distancing, and prohibited mixing with the children in other bubbles, keeping contagion at bay. This common-sense approach based on trust among the three groups allowed for consistency and reliability of "dancing with the Corona," to use their phrase, so that children could go back to school safely.

While in America, there were still two worlds, with no trust between the two camps. That's what happened to trust in this age of COVID.

The War for Trust

When the pandemic ran out of control in July of 2020, Trump continued to claim that he had done everything perfectly, that he had saved millions of lives by curtailing travel from China, and that everything was under control at this point, and that children should return to school. There was decreasing trust in him by many, but those likely suffering from the Dunning-Kruger Effect, his extremist base, still believed in him despite so much contradictory information from the infectious disease experts and the reality of an alarming increase in cases, not only in the US but all over Europe as well.

So, the dynamic of trust was completely bifurcated between the Trump base and the rest of the country. Though many followed the science path with rational thinking, others believed the opposite, some very strongly. Public health workers around the country began to retire early or just quit, sometimes because of the fear of death threats they were getting from Trump's strong supporters.

Things seemed to come to a head as far as trust was concerned as the pandemic began to run wild. At one point, Trump decided to attack the top public health officials, as a competition for trust became apparent. In an opinion piece in *USA Today*, Peter Navarro, assistant to Trump, wrote that the eminent epidemiologist, Dr. Anthony Fauci, "has been wrong about everything I have interacted with him on."[5] Dan Scavino, the Trump administration's deputy chief of staff for communications, posted a Ben Garrison cartoon to his Facebook page on July 12, 2020, showing Dr. Fauci as Dr Faucett, pouring cold water on Trump's plans. That's when the war for trust was on, and poor Dr. Fauci was caught in the crossfire.

By the time the pandemic began to slow down after the mass inoculations under Biden's watch, there was a pill on the horizon that could significantly keep infections down. Over three billion dollars of the $1.9 trillion coronavirus relief package Mr. Biden signed into law in March, 2021 would be allocated for research and development on this pill,[6] all this while the Delta variant was beginning to spread throughout the US.[7]

The race to beat SARS-CoV-2 was not over and may continue for some indeterminate amount of time. Scientists expected some variants to be even more dangerous than Delta, and they continued to plan on further research to battle whatever came down the road.[8]

Then came Omicron and the rules changed once again. Less deadly but much more contagious, there was confusion and fear, with a mixture of vigilance and indifference. "Omicron has turned, quickly, into something that is just different," said Dr. Allison Arwady, Chicago's top health official.[9]

At this point, it appeared that there was reason for optimism. Perhaps Omicron was the swan song for COVID-19—a variant that was more contagious yet remarkably less dangerous, at least for those already vaccinated. One cartoon by Shannon Wheeler, published in *The New Yorker*, had one female character asking another:

"Other than obsessive bread-making, compulsive cleaning, British-TV-baking-series bingeing, doom scrolling, stewing in self-pity, emotional breakdowns, solitary drinking, stalking of exes, online business meetings that parody actual work, and occasional violations of lockdown followed by guilt and self-recrimination and worried promises to do better, how were your last two years of pandemic isolation?"[10]

As if to say, well that seems to be over for now.

But fate cannot be blindsided. By the summer of 2022, the then-most recent variant, BA.5, was doing its work of infecting and reinfecting more and more victims. The arms race between virus and humans continued. Even Dr. Fauci himself was not immune, suffering reinfection.[11] The end of this pandemic was far from over at that point.

CHAPTER NINE

The Challenge of COVID-19: Reinfection and Vaccines

This is not over till it's over everywhere.

—Former British Prime Minister Gordon Brown, on CNN's Fareed Zakaria GPS, June 6, 2021

It's back to the issue of trust . . . you need to see that the vaccine is safe and effective.

—Kathleen Sebelius, former head of HHS

In sum, what ails us today is something that cannot be cured by a COVID-19 vaccine. We have lost the trust in each other and in our institutions and a basic sense of what is true—all necessary to navigate a health crisis together.

—Tom Friedman

My life was at stake. Whether to wear a mask or not. Whether to attend the party that promised safe distancing. Get that so desperately needed haircut. Go out for a bite at that new restaurant promising distancing and disposable menus. What to do? Whom to trust?

I was much better at this when home sheltering first started. I had fresh batteries. But their power has just worn out. I realize now, after so much social deprivation, how much I'm a social creature. I need to be with people, not only family, but friends, associates, new potential friendships, even strangers—just to walk among them, do some people watching. I could not help feeling, "I'm not going to live in fear. I will take my chances with the virus. I'm not going to stay home."

Maybe that is why the protests for Black Lives Matter were so popular so quickly and so pervasive after the George Floyd incident. Not to diminish the moral imperative to protest, but any excuse to get out of the house and *socialize* certainly helped motivate getting out to support the very worthy cause.

A (Very) Brief History of Pandemics

In 2012, Shi Zhengli, a scientist at Wuhan Institute of Virology, otherwise known as the "bat woman," reported to the world that there would be a bat-borne virus spilling over to humans sometime in the not-too-distant future, predicting the outbreak of SARS-CoV-2, causing the illness of COVID-19. Thought by many to originate in the stalls at Wuhan's Huanan seafood market, the predicted virus crossed the barrier to humans in mid-December of 2019. The first recorded victim was fifty-seven-year-old Wei Guixian, who sold shrimp from large buckets at the marketplace. The first American reported to be victim of this virus was a thirty-five-year-old man in Everett, Washington who had recently returned from visiting his family in Wuhan. And that is how the epidemic began, soon to become pandemic.

Before that was the H1N1 swine flu epidemic in 2009, followed by the Ebola outbreak in 2014. But the recorded history of epidemics reaches much further back.

The first-century Romans suffered from smallpox, then known as the Antonine Plague, killing up to 2,000 Roman citizens a day with a 25 percent mortality rate. This was soon followed by a disease starting in Constantinople and reaching out through the Mediterranean world. Killing thousands of helpless victims per day in the Byzantine Empire in the first century was the Plague of Justinian, brought on board ships by flea-ridden rats.

The first full pandemic was the Black Death in the mid-1300s, killing up to half the European population—about fifty million people. At the end of the nineteenth century came the first modern pandemic that was carried through the world by modern transport such as railway and faster ships. This was the Russian flu, caused by Influenza A, and killing over a million individuals.

Then came three more pandemics at the turn of the century: the third plague pandemic, caused by Yersinia pestis, carried by flea-ridden rats once again, beginning in southwest China, traveling through Hong Kong, India, and Indonesia, killing over ten million; then cholera, killing over 800,000 in India and then Indonesia, still not totally eradicated; followed by the 1918 Spanish flu, a form of H1N1, killing over fifty million.

Within the past fifty years, we've been challenged by the Asian flu (H2N2), the Hong Kong flu (H3N2) and, most recently, HIV/AIDS, killing thirty-two million, with about thirty-eight million currently living with highly effective medical treatment. And now we are faced with the current pandemic, SARS-CoV-2, known as COVID-19. When it was too new for us to have definitive information about it, we didn't yet know whether infection leads to long-lasting immunity.

As soon as China became aware of COVID-19, they published its genome for the world to see. By Jan 13, 2020, the researchers at Moderna were at work beginning to design an mRNA molecule to recognize the virus and defend against it. The testing was difficult and over sixteen million got infected. More than 300,000 Americans died before it got approved. But that is what it takes to ensure the safety of those who receive it.

If President Trump had not been so politically motivated to suppress the dangers of SARS-CoV-2, there might have been more precautions earlier on and the trust level might not have fallen so low when the truth did come out. Since the pandemic affected everyone, trust was a major issue.

Infected? Again?

And then came the ultimate trust issue: could you be reinfected with COVID-19 once you have gotten it? Whom to trust on that critical issue?

The stories started around July 2020. Some studies indicated that it was indeed possible, that there had been some cases that proved it.

At least without reinfection, there would be the ultimate back-up scenario of herd immunity. But, with reinfection, that would never be possible. And, with an effective vaccine taking years to produce, would we be doomed to this phobia about human contact for another year or two, or three? Locked in our shelters, dying of boredom, watching way too much TV, too stressed out to enjoy reading, living one ground-hog day after another?

Early Accounts

According to a story reported by Fox 11 in Los Angeles, in April 2020, a woman named Mary had a sore throat, got tested, and was positive. She did what she was supposed to do: she took care of herself, got over it, and tested negative in May.

Then, at the end of June, Mary felt much sicker than before, had trouble breathing, was taken to the emergency room, tested positive again, and was kept at the hospital for two weeks.

"I was following the orders since the beginning of March . . . wearing a mask, I was doing the gloves, the hand sanitizer. I was doing everything right . . . what did I do wrong?" she asked, holding back tears.

Dr. Stuart Ditchek, a New Jersey physician, reported, "We now have two cases that are reinfected that I am personally connected with." One of his patients had tested positive a few months earlier, then went to a party following which she tested positive once more. Another patient from the same family reported a similar reinfection after seven weeks of testing negative.

What were we to make of these accounts? When confronted with such cases, most of the experts expressed cynicism. Whom should we trust? How many of us have had doubts about doctors treating our medical problems who have said one thing, but that changed when we checked with another physician for a second opinion? That's under normal circumstances. Now we had an issue that, beyond the usual medical challenges, involved our survival in this dangerous environment. Trust became even more delicate in this Age of Misinformation.

Long Live the Virus

Epidemiological research suggested other, more intriguing possibilities. One was that there might be a prolonged reaction to the virus that included periods of testing negative. Some proposed that this was because of testing error. "I haven't heard of a case where it's [reinfection] been truly unambiguously demonstrated," said Marc Lipsitch, an epidemiologist at the Harvard T.H. Chan School of Public Health.[1]

Other possible explanations were even more concerning. According to Dr. Robbiani of Rockefeller University, people could respond to the coronavirus in different ways, though all do form some level of antibodies.[2]

Some tests are so sensitive that they may be picking up information from very minute remnants of the virus, even a single viral molecule. By comparison, Dr. Wen-Hsuan Lin of Johns Hopkins University found that genetic evidence of the measles virus RNA can persist in the blood, respiratory tract, or lymph nodes four to five times longer than the infectious virus itself, and a rebound phase can show a viral load of up ten times higher than the original count before leveling off again.[3]

In a study by Takuya Sekine and his associates, the data revealed that even asymptomatic and mild cases of COVID-19 result in T cells with good memory for defense.[4] Yet, according to another group of Chinese researchers, those who were asymptomatic for COVID-19 had antibodies that tended to disappear within two months.[5] Another group of scientists in the Wanzhou District of China reported that those who were asymptomatic had a weaker immune response than those who did have symptoms. So, there are different accounts of the length of immunity following infection.[6]

Though up to 80 percent of those infected with COVID-19 are symptom-free (purportedly the younger ones), those who do suffer mild symptoms but enough to bring them to a hospital have a very strong immune response involving several components: increased antibody-secreting cells, follicular T-helper cells, activated CD4+ and CD8+ T cells and IgM/IgG SARS-CoV-2-binding antibodies. This may be more than you'd ever want to know but it does help understand the breadth and depth of the immune response to the mid-level range of symptomatology. Irani Thevarajan and her colleagues observed this in their forty-seven-year-old patient, with the immune factors persisting for a full seven days after symptomatic recovery.[7]

"Lull" between Stages or Test Imperfections?

Another case of reinfection was thirty-seven-year-old Megan Kent, who lost her sense of smell and taste but otherwise felt fine. Her boyfriend was positive and that's how she became infected. She let the illness run its course with few other symptoms and then returned to work a couple weeks later at Melrose Wakefield Hospital.

In May, she felt immensely fatigued and went to the hospital thinking she had a case of mononucleosis. Guess what! Here was another case of presumed reinfection, only "a hundred times worse," she explained. She stayed sick for a month this time.

Some doctors found it hard to accept the reinfection scenario. They speculated that the interim between the two "infections" might just be a lull between two symptomatic stages, with a low count of viral levels between the two. Add to this the known shortcomings of testing accuracy and you have a case of a single infection being wrongly diagnosed as reinfection.

Yet reinfection cases continued to haunt the researchers, according to a Reuters report. In the Sichuan province's Chengdu city, a patient was diagnosed as being reinfected after being discharged and returning home.[8] Even there, one expert blamed poor testing. So, no clear answer here. Dr. Lei Xuezhong argued that tests should involve testing material from the lungs rather than the nose, where the virus might not be as detectable.

More evidence of reinfection came from the Far East once again. Dr. Lan Lan of the Zhongnan Hospital of Wuhan University in Wuhan found that four of her colleagues were reinfected after being released from the hospital based on the absence of clinical symptoms and radiological abnormalities and two negative RT-PCR test results.[9] A colleague, Dr. X. Xie, surmised that false-negative RT-PCR test results could have been the factor that led to the belief in reinfection in this study.[10]

So, we were back to the divide between those who thought that reinfection was the case and those who believed that it was more likely a case of poor testing and the variations in intensity of the original infection. So much, according to some, depended on the accuracy and quality of the testing protocol.

Another issue related to reinfection was in the realm of mutations of the virus. Dr. Korber and her colleagues found one significant mutation, which they referred to as Spike D614G, which began spreading in Europe in early February 2020.[11] The researchers had not yet found any significant change in transmissibility or fatality with this mutation but merely pointed out that the mutations do take place and can be a warning of future differences as time passes. But common sense tells us that mutations may make reinfection more of a possibility.

So Many Questions

On another note, Dr. Alba Grifoni at the La Jolla Institute for Immunology pointed to the fact that some people were less symptomatic of COVID-19 because they already had immunity (in the form of memory T cells) to the common cold virus, because of similarities between the two viruses. Even in the absence of antibodies, the immune cells against the common cold can also act against COVID-19 according to Grifoni and her associates,[12] and this was corroborated by Alessandrao Sette and Shane Crotty at the same Institute.[13] This type of pre-existing cross-immunity has been known for at least a decade.[14,15,16]

There is still so much unknown about this new virus that will keep us guessing for quite a while. Do the infections stay hidden like the herpes virus to spring up when we're more stressed and fatigued? Will we ever be free of the virus, or will it keep its position of stealth to re-emerge when we are least expecting it? We do seem to have data indicating that asymptomatic cases result in the least amount of immunity. Does that mean that there is some relationship between severity of symptoms and consequent immunity? If so, for how long?

All these details may be more than you wanted to know but, since there is so much at stake in terms of our ultimate health, I chose to share this information with you so you can decide on your own level of trust about these complex issues. Details help determine trust. Scientists often disagree as they search for the right answers. That's what science is all about.

In terms of COVID-19, there are still questions about the accuracy of testing results, and whether the virus can hide out in the body and reappear with a vengeance later. Whatever the answer, the public can feel confused and frightened by the lack of certainty. Whom to trust remains a challenge, especially in this Age of Misinformation.

With questions remaining about this virus, it is not surprising that the issue of trust continues to challenge. Where there is uncertainty, simple solutions strive for acceptance. There are those who are more scientifically inclined and follow the data, as opposed to those who fall into the political realm, preferring easy solutions and freedom from the three Ws. As a matter of observation, there are many who still believe that COVID-19 is a hoax. "They just want to say that the disease is nothing more than a cold," focusing on those who are asymptomatic or show only light symptoms.

The truth is that we know much less than we wish we could know. Aside from the grim prospect of new pandemics, due to higher degrees of interaction between humans and other animals affected by climate change,[17] there remains the possibility, even probability, many say, that variants and subvariants will continue to haunt us.[18] In the spring of 2023, there was concern that the bird flu H5N1 might move from birds to humans but the occurrence was quite rare.[19]

CHAPTER TEN

The Various Variants

Future pandemics aren't hypothetical; they're inevitable and imminent. As rising temperatures force animals to relocate, species that have never coexisted will meet, allowing the viruses within them to find new hosts—humans included. Dealing with all of this again is a matter of when, not if.

—Ed Yong, in *The Atlantic*, 2022.

The use of masks was very controversial, especially for school children where some were required to wear masks at school all day. One parent was reported to say, "The teachers won't be teaching. They'll be trying to get the children to wear their masks. And keeping children six feet apart all day? Impossible!" or "Wearing a mask all day isn't good for you—breathing your own air and germs all day doesn't make sense."

By mid-June 2020, a benchmark of ten million cases worldwide had been reached. The former president of Brazil, Jair Bolsonaro, showed no interest in getting his citizens vaccinated, despite the World Health Organization warning that the worst was yet to come. Food delivery to hungry citizens was becoming an issue not only in Brazil, but also in such areas as Africa, the mid-East, and South Asia.

Yet, despite this concern, the official US position began to shift toward opening the economy, restoring business to restaurants and cafés. A yen for travel threatened to open a pent-up demand.

Most popular is the quote from former *Wheel of Fortune* game show host, Chuck Woolery, who is a definite advocate of the political realm. On July 12, 2020, he tweeted: "The most outrageous lies are the ones about COVID-19. Everyone is lying. The CDC, media, Democrats, our doctors, not all but most, that we are told to trust."[1] Trust seems to have disappeared here. What ever happened to trust?

Over a month later, the day before the Republican Convention, the White House announced a milestone advance against COVID-19 in terms of convalescent plasma. Most scientists were concerned that the data from earlier that week, when the FDA indicated more testing was necessary, about the wisdom of rushing this "treatment" ahead. If the treatment was now available to everyone, the opportunity to test it scientifically was no longer there. This became a very critical example of whom to trust, the president who needed a political shot in the arm for the next day's convention, or the scientists who were dismayed that the chance to test the treatment was disappearing.

A study at King's College in England explored the issue of reinfection and concluded that there were still no confirmed cases of COVID-19 reinfection anywhere in the world at the time.[20] COVID-19 does have some resemblance to SARS and, to a lesser extent, MERS. So far, there were no reports of reinfection of SARS and only one reported incident of MERS reinfection.[2] Though there was a report out of Hong Kong of the first case of reinfection confirmed by genome sequencing, the scientists maintained that the thirty-three-year-old man showed no symptoms, and that the reinfection just increased his immunity to anything more serious than he had already experienced.[3] This was the first confirmed case of reinfection, according to the scientists, out of twenty-three million documented cases. And then came the first documented case in the US in late August of 2020, a twenty-five-year-old man from Nevada who was reinfected forty-eight days after his initial infection.[4] Given the history of millions of cases around the world, the scientists were not surprised. It was an exceedingly rare event.

Where We've Gone Wrong

In an article in The Atlantic, Ed Yong[5] pointed out that there are nine fallacies that keep us from solving the pandemic issue:

1) Rather than approach the pandemic in holistic fashion, we entertain one "solution" after another until it fails, and we move on to the next, e.g., hydroxychloroquine, convalescent plasma, dexamethasone, remdesivir.

2) Engaging in false dichotomies, we separate the slightly affected from the severely affected, rather than looking at the more complex spectrum of illness from asymptomatic to severely affected, leaving out the "long-haulers," who suffer for months; we separate the sheltering solution from opening up, rather than opening up with strict adherence to the three Ws while going back to work and school. (The National Hockey League has done something similar by keeping all their players "bubbled" away from the larger population during their playoff season.)

3) We fall in love with certain preventive measures in "theatrical" fashion while not looking closely at their efficacy, e.g., the highly theatrical show of scrubbing and bleaching large areas when we know that most of the contagion comes from breathing near others rather than touching surfaces.

4) We focus on placing blame on those individuals who go out and infect others rather than looking at systemic approaches that can decrease contagion overall. Overcrowded prisons and understaffed nursing homes are just as bad as crowded restaurants and bars, where we have more control than we are comfortable using.

5) We hope that normalcy will return soon automatically without being realistic about the time necessary for validating the efficacy of any vaccines under consideration (especially by

the past administration). Some of us just give up, pretending that the pandemic is a political hoax against Trump, a form of psychological, or even subconscious, denial.

6) Similarly, we entertain "magical thinking" about quick cures that are just not scientifically justifiable, like Trump's declaring that the pandemic will just magically disappear with the changing season, or that we have it totally under control despite statistics to the contrary.

7) There are some physicians in those areas hit later who seem naive to the strident contagion of the pandemic, just because they haven't witnessed it firsthand. As Yong puts it, "They seem to forget that viruses spread." For reasons that may be largely political, the US lagged behind other countries, many of them developing nations, in taking charge earlier and more effectively.

8) Some remain in a "reactive rut" who seem to have just given up, resigned to a new normal that we just accept. More critical is the reactive rut that our past administration had in hiding the facts to "avoid panic." Bob Woodward was able to prove that clearly in his taping of Trump when the latter said that he intentionally "played down" the facts, resulting in one of the world's greatest disasters that could have been avoided.

9) On a very troubling note, just like this last point, is the "habituation of horror," where we are no longer concerned about the terrible catastrophe that the pandemic brings to bear. We have gotten used to it and become too complacent. As Ed Yong put it, "Like poverty and racism, school shootings and police brutality, mass incarceration and sexual harassment, widespread extinctions and changing climate, COVID-19 might become yet another unacceptable thing that America comes to accept."[5]

The Vaccine We Were Waiting For

At the end of the day—or pandemic—everyone was waiting for the vaccine to end it all—well not quite everyone. There were those who had their doubts. According to Barry Bloom, former Dean of the Harvard Chan School of Public Health, because of the mixed signals we've all been getting, about hydroxychloroquine for instance, there are the vaccination skeptics, even more than the usual. Trust is essential for vaccines to work.[6]

"Without trust," said Bloom, "a vaccine doesn't do much good in the world." He and his colleagues believed that only 50 percent would accept a vaccine according to the then-current polls. And with the attempts by the past administration to promise a "fast lane" to a successful vaccine, skepticism just increased. Such skepticism could block the effectiveness of even the safest vaccines. Successful research on such vaccines "typically involves tens of thousands of subjects."[7] Then there was the challenge of distribution. First came such obvious populations as nursing home residents, health care workers and vulnerable groups like prison inmates. At the next level would be those most likely to spread contagion, like youngsters and essential workers—then the rest. "Without trust, however," according to the *Harvard Gazette*, even those within the selected demographics may not universally embrace a vaccine."[8]

Trump did not help any when he directly contradicted the head of CDC on claims as to when a vaccine might be ready. Dr. Robert Redfield, under oath, told a Senate committee on September 17 not to expect distribution of a vaccine till mid-2021 at the earliest. When Trump was questioned about this a few hours later that day, he replied, "I think he made a mistake when he said that. It's just incorrect information," and insisted that the vaccine would be available prior to the election, saying, "under no circumstances will it be as late as the doctor said."[9]

That same day, Trump himself was confronted by two vaccine

research companies—Moderna, with 30,000 participants, and Pfizer, with 44,000—sharing their data with the public, a highly unusual decision. Moderna claimed that the earliest their vaccine might be available would be mid-2021, while Pfizer's chief executive reported they would not even have any information on that until the following month.[10]

Lacking Trust

In fact, trust in the vaccine had declined about 20 percent between May and September when measured across gender, age, ethnicity, and education. About half said they'd probably get the vaccine if it were available, down from 72 percent in May. Both cost and uncertainty about side effects were factors. Seventy-eight percent were concerned that the vaccine might be pushed into distribution too fast.[11]

But Governor Andrew Cuomo was not following the crowd when it came to trusting vaccine readiness, especially with the appearance of a second wave of infections in Europe. On September 24, 2020, he said: "Frankly, I'm not going to trust the federal government's opinion."[12]

One of the pervasive challenges was the pushback that so many people had in terms of their trust of public health advocacy. Dr. Bruce Miller, writing in *The Journal of the American Medical Association*, pointed out how many people resisted the information that was available. "The US public health response to coronavirus disease 2019 (COVID-19) has been dismal, characterized by antimask behavior, antivaccine beliefs, conspiracy theories about the origins of COVID-19, and vocal support by elected officials for unproven therapies," he claimed.[13] As time went by, there was still so much more to be learned about COVID-19, especially about the role of the T cells.[14] Although most believe that the vaccines were stopping the spread,[15] some believed that despite this, remnants of it might remain for years and years.[16] So what was a public health official to do? Just fight the good fight until it was all over?

By March 2021, President Biden promised that there would be sufficient vaccines to service all Americans as vaccines became more and more available.[17] But the darker side of the issue remained with the arrival of variants with unknown character,[18] with B.1.1.7 being of special concern because of its more highly contagious nature.[19] Sadly, it turns out, such variants often result when immunocompromised patients harbor the virus for longer periods than normal, allowing the virus to evolve within a patient with time on its side,[20,21] as the patient is given sequences of medication, giving the wild virus an opportunity to evolve into variants that are less susceptible to available treatments.[22]

In early 2021, the race between vaccination and the variants that were appearing to threaten domination over the original strain became a bothersome issue. It was becoming clear that enduring problems were unavoidable. At the least, annual boosters would likely become necessary, just as for the common flu. Herd immunity seemed like the most possible resolution.[23]

Finally, on a more positive note, it seemed as if it was possible to contain the virus through discipline consistently applied throughout a region. Toward the latter part of 2020, with 400,000 dead from COVID-19 in the US and over 1.1 million worldwide,[24] New York State went from the most afflicted state to the healthiest, hovering at about a 1 percent positivity rate while it was up to 13 percent in the Miami-Dade area of Florida and up to 15 percent in Houston.[25]

By late Spring 2021, there were many more cases of COVID-19 than had been expected. Because of the explosive outbreak in India and South America, the count was as high as 825,000, India accounting for a full 43 percent of cases globally,[26] with 3,600 new deaths reported daily in India.[27] But in the US, the numbers were looking much better. By then over half of all Americans had received at least one shot of the vaccine. "We're clearly turning the corner," said Michael Osterholm, director of the Center for Infectious Disease Research and Policy at the University of Minnesota.[28]

One interesting sideline was the revelation that the virus had ethnic preferences, relating to racial genotypes, specifically the angiotensin-converting enzyme, *ACE1* II. Those with this genotype, Asians, are less likely to suffer from SARS-CoV-2[29] and less likely to die from such infection than Europeans.[30] It is difficult to determine whether much of obesity is genetic or due to lifestyle factors. Along with the findings that obese Blacks and Hispanics are more prone to the serious effects of COVID-19, some researchers continue to focus on obesity as an ethnic factor affecting susceptibility.[31]

Another concern was the growing number of variants that could be brewing in these high-count countries that would eventually be traveling to the US. At one point, the South African variant, B.1.351, was reinfecting some who had already had the virus, as reported in South Carolina and Maryland. The UK variant, B.1.1.7, 30 percent more lethal than the original virus, was found in thirty states. The Brazilian variant, P.1, was found in Minnesota. University of Minnesota epidemiologist Michael Osterholm was warning of a hurricane effect caused by all these variants.[32] And then there was the AY.4.2 Delta variant first discovered in the UK, even more contagious than its predecessor.[33]

According to a consolidation of ongoing research from the White House in the fall of 2021, "future biological threats could be far worse" and "serious biological threats will occur at an increasing frequency."[34]

Yet when we heard of fortuitous medications that were found to be helpful, such as the antidepressant, Fluvoxamine, there was hope that over time we'd gain more control over these terrible viruses.[35]

When it turned out that the US, despite its wealth and scientific achievements, was doing more poorly than most other developed countries in terms of fighting the pandemic, it turned out there were at least two factors for that: 1) because of its assurance that it had the money and knowhow to deal with this deadly virus, it did not take the early stages as seriously as other countries, believing it would have the last say in terms of some vaccine that was yet to be developed by its scientists. 2) Because of its wealth and the lifestyle to which its citizens were accustomed, there was more obesity prevalent than in less wealthy countries, making its citizens more susceptible. But since most Americans have either been infected or had vaccinations, or both, serious outcomes were less frequent.[36]

By the end of 2022, one thing became clear: vaccines did help and those who avoided them, like many Republicans, on political grounds, were dying more frequently than their Democratic counterparts—76 percent higher.[37]

Apart from politics, it appeared that there were two groups: those younger folks who "seem to have tuned out COVID . . . as a minor nuisance," and those over fifty who made up over 90 percent of all COVID-related deaths. By the end of 2022, during which there were over 230,000 COVID-related deaths in America, there was a "split between the high-risk minority and the low-risk majority," according to Yasmin Tayag, writing the *The Atlantic*.[38] To protect everyone, she recommended, after looking at all the research, "avoid getting infected" by masking up in crowded places and before seeing older relatives. By the end of 2022, when the variants B.Q.1 and B.Q.1.1 were at 44 percent of all infections, Pfizer's bivalent booster provided more than five times the neutralizing antibodies as the original vaccine, providing substantial protection against serious illness and death.[39]

The scientific approach does work. All you need to do is apply it . . . if you trust it.

And now for a bit of humorous relief:

A is for absolutely nothing getting done.
B is for boredom.
C is for the covidiots.
D is for "doing our best."

E is for extra time at home.
F is for my father who died without a visit from me.
G is for grim milestones.
H is for heart-heavy numbers.
I is for inoculation, a word misused.
J is for Jack in the Box drive-through, the only place we eat out now.
K is for knowing someone who died of Covid.
L is for living simply.
M is for meals at home.
N is for never going out unmasked.
O is for outdoor eating in the cold.
P is for pandemic.
Q is for quirky Zoom weddings and funerals.
R is for relatives who don't understand my fear.
S is for sick and tired of this.
T is for ticking time bomb.
U is for unprecedented.
V is for vaccines versus variants.
W is for wanting my shot.
X is for X-rays of Covid lungs.
Y is for yelling at strangers who get too close.
Z is for zoonotic.

—Margaret "Page" Kakowski, Portland, Oregon[40]

Finally, there is the question of more pandemics in our near or (hopefully) distant futures.[41] If they do come, we need to be as prepared as possible.[42,43]

We must be alert to all that is necessary to keep pandemics at bay. As Bill Gates put it, "The world must take action now to make sure COVID-19 becomes the last pandemic, and one of the biggest moves we can make is to support the world's principal health experts—the W.H.O."[44]

At the time of this writing, we had the variant XBB.1.5 leading in the US, followed by XBB.1.9.1. But in India and increasingly in the US, there is a new interloper, XBB.1.16, refereed to as Arcturus, clocking in at 7 percent of all COVID-19 cases nation-wide at this point, reported by the W.H.O.[45] When will it all end?

In the meantime, here is an approach to surviving the next attack that brings us from fear and stress to confidence and a sense of empowerment.

RADICAL STRATEGIES: OUR RESPONSE TO SHELTERING AT HOME DUE TO COVID-19 VARIANTS OR ANY FUTURE PANDEMIC

What National and Local Governments Can Do:

Health issues: Through national and local TV and print media ads, government can earn our trust and promote the benefits of proven health activities:

- Trusting the well-known three Ws: wearing masks, washing hands, and watching distance.
- Educating people to recognize the adverse outcomes associated with the preexisting effect of underlying health issues, including obesity, to the consequences of infection.
- Identifying the data that reveal how people of color may be more prone to underlying health factors.
- Addressing the impact of unequal access to health resources for those dealing with poverty and the role of the health system to prevent disproportionate outcomes.

What Local Community Organizations, Including Community Centers, Religious Organizations, and Nursing Homes, Can Do:

Support: Encourage mutual support for these efforts in pairs or small groups who can become

> sufficiently trustworthy to one another and accountable with positive feedback.

Grieving: Provide opportunities for individuals to access online communities developed precisely for the purpose of supporting those who have lost loved ones to the pandemic. When we've lost loved ones, grieving can be a very lonely experience.

Sheltering: Provide programs that recognize and assist with the hardships of sheltering at home that include:

- A sense of isolation and loneliness.
- Growing pandemic fatigue due to worry and stress as time passes.
- Increases in family conflict, sometimes leading to physical abuse.
- The growing possibility of what psychiatrists refer to as post-traumatic stress disorder (PTSD).
- A growing sense of doom as the pandemic continues with no clear end in sight and no definitive information on the availability of an effective vaccine that will end our suffering.

What Individuals Can Do on Their Own, on a Personal Basis:

How to deal with these challenges:
- To overcome the sense of isolation and loneliness, create and join online support networks relating to the pandemic that are trustworthy.
- To overcome pandemic fatigue, learn (online) such concepts as time management and life-path planning. By scheduling your activities, you can use your time more meaningfully:

- [ ] to catch up on books waiting to be read
- [ ] to learn new skills through YouTube and other sites
- [ ] to cut out some time for physical exercise that can be done at home, such as yoga, push-ups, stretching exercises, etc.
- [ ] to make time to contact friends and family for ongoing connection on a scheduled basis
- [ ] to look forward to a joyfully prepared lunch or dinner and sharing that mutual experience online with friends or family doing the same, through Zoom or Skype, for example.
- [ ] to use your time for further career development through online classes. Life-path planning can be included.
- [ ] Time management allows for all these planned activities, which transform isolation into a sense of power in improving life experience, even while sheltering.

- **Family conflict** can become an issue when families are bunched together over months. Couples and families begin to reveal their previously hidden needs, whether for more attention or more living space or privacy. This is the time to learn how conflict resolution works (online again). Such skills enable individuals to learn what their housemates (roommate, spouse, partner, siblings, parents, children) really feel about being cooped up and then reveal what they would like changed, starting with very small requests. Assertiveness skills (again learned online) are also very helpful, learning how to ask for one's needs being met in an empathic and supportive style.

Finally, after learning what your housemates enjoy as activities, there can be an effort to spend some time engaging in games or friendly competitions involving such mutually enjoyable activities. All this could tone down the necessity of living together without family conflict.

- To avoid PTSD, it's very helpful to be able to identify those aggravating aspects of sheltering and proactively avoid such stressors if possible. This may involve some of the other skills, such as assertiveness training and conflict resolution. In part, this involves learning to identify feelings of stress and then, as precisely as possible, how to label them with a trusting and reassuring demeanor. Once this is done, they can be discussed with supportive housemates as well.

- To overcome a sense of doom about the length of recovery, there is the option to set priorities that do take time one has, lots of it, to achieve lifetime goals, such as
    - ☐ losing weight and improving your health
    - ☐ taking online courses to further your career opportunities
    - ☐ learning a foreign language
    - ☐ writing the book you've always threatened to do while your friends rolled their eyes (your own autobiography!)
    - ☐ learning a new craft or skill through YouTube by which you might be able to earn a living or even enjoy when that period or so of sheltering is finally up.

As well, it sometimes takes time to get your primary relationship back to where it was when you first committed to it with mutual support and trust. This is as good a time as any to devote time to this pleasurable challenge.

> Finally, this is an excellent time to devote a little bit of your energy to reconnect with whatever form of spirituality you enjoy, whether it's a religious organization, some informal group, or meditation on your own.

The challenge of COVID-19 has hit all of us, whether we don masks or not, whether we've been infected or not, whether our loved ones support our efforts or not. If another dangerous subvariant emerges, or as we consider the likelihood of future pandemics, these responses give us some arrows to fight back, at least in some small, personal way, giving us a sense of control over our lives when we need it most, until we get sufficient relief from vaccines and other successful treatments.

OVERVIEW AND UPDATE

Innovation is what will get us out of this.

—Bill Gates

The Right Author for This Book

Why was I the right author for a book like this? Because of my proven ability to take diverse issues and bring them into a single focus that can be addressed. I've proven this in the many professional articles and books I've already published.

- *Dreams That Come True* (Doubleday) took different dream theories and analyzed them to create a successful approach to making your dreams focus on a topic of concern, create a thoughtful question about, and answer to, that issue, and then give some practical and useful tips on what it would take to resolve the issue.[1] This approach has been applied to many clients and it works every single time. In *4 Global Crises*, I use a similar approach to bring helpful recommendations for dealing with each of the four global challenges. Perhaps most critical is the approach used to resolve international conflict to avoid nuclear threat.

- In *Look 10 Years Younger/Live 10 Years Longer* (Prentice Hall), I examined the various approaches to healthy lifestyle—smart eating, exercise habits, stress reduction, cardiac awareness, and positive interpersonal relationships—to develop a system to look younger and live longer.[2] All these diverse components were forged into a single, healthier lifestyle that includes the overarching dynamic of trust, which is so crucial to interpersonal communication in any context. In *4 Global Crises*, I offer readers novel approaches to take control and manage their anxieties and stresses.

- In *Putting Emotional Intelligence to Work* (Butterworth-Heinemann), I took all the theories of leadership and open communication he could get my hands on, forged them into the framework of emotional intelligence and came up with an approach to "bringing out the best talents in our executives and managers," according to Andreas Renschler, then CEO and president of Mercedes Benz US International.[3] In *4 Global Crises*, I utilize a similar approach, presenting various skills that can be applied to the readers' everyday lives whether in business, education, or even politics.

- In *Love Sex and Passion for the Rest of Your Life: How to Create the Ultimate Relationship* (Humanics), I combined the many theories of love communication to create, "one of those rare books that balances information with inspiration and insight with practical suggestions," according to the best-selling author of *1001 Ways to Be Romantic*, Gregory J.P. Godek.[4] In this book, *4 Global Crises*, I offer readers well-researched, factual, detailed and balanced information, combining them in order to conquer your fears and stresses about the four global challenges.

- In *ConnectAbility* (McGraw-Hill), I wrote about the neuroscience of sharing power with others, and how to match skills with the challenges at hand. I wrote about fusing integrity with an open approach to humor, as well as dealing with emotions with more awareness. By combining all these factors effectively, I show proof—backed by academic research—that all this, done effectively, will result in higher income, less turnover in organizations, greater job satisfaction, and greater leadership and management skills.[5] I also do the same for concerns about new pandemic variants (how to quarantine, when necessary, with greater emotional awareness of others, i.e., family members) and social injustice (how to lead others into creating community support).

- In *Secrets of a Zen Millionaire* (Motivational Press), I selected important Eastern philosophies, combined them with proven approaches to investment, and forged these insights into a failsafe plan to build personal wealth, and have a more fulfilling life at the same time. The subtitle was *Living More Happily and Getting Rich by Doing the Right Thing*. One highly successful consultant and author of *Leading at the Edge of Chaos,* Daryl Conner, wrote that the book did a "great job of bridging Eastern philosophy with financial acumen. I've never seen this union before . . . well done!" Another corporate consultant, C. Richard Weylman, wrote: "Artfully written, it provides each reader with the pathway to a fulfilling life—financially, emotionally and yes, even spiritually."[6] In this book on the four global challenges, I share how doing the right thing involves taking responsibility for keeping the planet healthier, and how bridging different philosophies can help prevent international conflict.

I was the right author for this book because I possess a unique ability to unite seemingly disparate factors into a successful approach that can resolve them all. In *4 Global Crises*, I tackle the four horsemen of the current apocalypse—climate change, pandemics, social injustice, nuclear threats—and offer a practical approach to transforming uncertainty and fear into an assertive, rational approach to each one of them.

Practical Resolutions to Four Global Crises

When I first began this book, concern about nuclear conflict seemed to take a back seat compared to the COVID-19 pandemic, climate change, and social injustice. But in late February of 2022, when Russia invaded Ukraine, the West's fears of nuclear conflict abruptly became much more relevant, especially to Europeans, neighbors of the warring countries who remembered all too well what global conflict can engender. This fourth horseman of the current apocalypse—the possibility of nuclear conflict—suddenly appeared much more threatening than before.

Then I became interested in how, after years of neglect—neglect of Earth's environment, neglect of minorities who suffered the injustice that's so ingrained in our culture, neglect of a new virus that was allowed to become a pandemic, neglect of the manipulations of social media on our values and choices—we could finally take control of the matters that are so crucial to our current culture and renew our sense of trust. All this has created what some refer to as the Age of Misinformation.

In order that you might feel less stressed and less victimized by events of this magnitude and can gain a greater sense of confidence and control, I offer some practical suggestions and powerful tools to help you gain a sense of taking charge with a new interactive approach. With your own personal response to each of these issues, you'll feel less stress and anxiety and a greater sense of optimism.

Our Urgent Crises: Beached Whales, Final Gasps, and Dirty Politics

Beached whales flailing in their heaviness, escaping the overbearing man-made auditory assault echoing in the ocean . . .

A policeman's knee pressing firmly against the neck of George Floyd as he gasps "Mama" with his final breaths . . . Less than three years later, an hour-long video revealed how Tyre Nichols was beaten to death by five police officers after a routine traffic stop.

The graves of pandemic victims, lying endlessly side by side, as seen from a bird's-eye view, with no one in sight to tend to these poor souls . . .

Videos of bombs exploding into residential areas and photos of devastation throughout Ukraine. . .

Take a closer look. What's the reality behind this montage of disasters? Are we humans responsible for the challenges of nature occurring all around us, what the media calls *climate change*? Are racial issues any worse than they've been for decades since the Civil Rights movement in the 1960s and '70s? Now that COVID-19 is falling into our rearview mirror, with a less lethal Omicron variant, XBB.1.5 (at the time of this writing), is it still worth so much of our attention? We're getting along so well with social media—why not just enjoy that modern luxury without having to attack it for no reason?

Here's what happened with the beached whales:

According to Anthony Hulse, author of *Cries from the Deep*:

> On August 11th, 2010, NOAA [the National Oceanic and Atmospheric Administration] gave permission for the US Navy to continue their training, which included mid and high-frequency sonar and the use of explosives, thus ignoring the devastating impact on marine life. They attempted to justify their actions by claiming sonar exposure is merely a matter of annoyance to whale and dolphins.[7]

The whales, apparently, felt differently. They couldn't withstand the noxious noise to their sensitive ears. They were forced to leave their normal environment and chose to escape the punishment by beaching themselves, where they would die of inner suffocation, unable to be moved. Similar threats to other species becoming extinct because of human exploitation of our planet—both on land and water—force us to consider whether we can trust our government to acknowledge and legislate sufficiently strong laws to protect our planet, as the former administration failed to do, but which US Special Presidential Envoy for Climate John Kerry hopes to accomplish.

At the global level, there are over ten million premature deaths due to fine particulate matter across the world.[8]

George Floyd has come to represent legions of minorities across the globe—across the United States, China, throughout India, within most countries of Africa. Systemic injustice has been revealed, percolating through social media. Can we trust our courts to mete out justice without prejudice to all members of society?

A few years later, another iconic incident occurred, when five police officers murdered twenty-nine-year-old Tyre Nichols by beating him to death, gloating about it by sending photos of the victim to friends while waiting for medical assistance, laughing and fist-bumping one another.

The pandemic, hopefully being tamed soon, has revealed just how vulnerable we all are as we learn that it's just a matter of time till the next one comes to threaten us. Will it be worse, killing off many more than the roughly 1 percent contaminated by COVID-19? Can we trust vaccines newly developed to quicken the demise of this deadly virus and the unknown variants to come?

Once Putin's aggression into Ukraine made us much more aware of nuclear conflict, old fears were dramatically renewed. So, how can we take charge of that issue? In the first section of this book, I went into greater detail about an approach to conflict resolution that is the basis of all good negotiation. Listening skills are important, of course, but the approach we've explored requires a depth of knowledge about its development and the confidence to go to extremes to make the process highly intimate though full of risk. It pays off when the process is done with the necessary courage to take the challenge and bring the necessary skills to bear.

What We have Learned

- Climate change presents challenges to which we can respond, such as making personal commitments to consume more wisely and mindfully and to electing responsible government.
- To cope with pandemic challenges, present and future, the process of quarantining can be made more productive, meaningful, and nurturing to self and others—and therefore less daunting.
- For systemic injustice, social networks can replace the numbing sense of victimhood with self-esteem and mutual support—rendering it less debilitating.
- Finally, to avoid nuclear threats, a deep process of facilitation skills for leading international negotiations exists that has been proven in the field by pioneers such as Dr. Carl Rogers[9] and President Jimmy Carter.

What Can We Trust?

At the end of 2020, the US experienced its most serious cyberattack by the Russians,[10] tantamount to a Pearl Harbor attack, according to most cybersecurity gurus.[11] Russia's sophisticated cyber-spy Foreign Intelligence Service, the SVR, was the aggressor, having obtained access to over 250 government networks, including the Homeland Security Agency, satellite sensors, targeting systems, and more.[12] Even back in 2016, most experts on social media believed that Putin's manipulation of social media aided significantly in Trump's victory over Hillary Clinton.[13] Can we trust our governments to ensure our national integrity and safety? Especially after the release of classified information by 21-year-old Air National Guardsman, Jack Teixeira in April of 2023?

Equally threatening are the effects of social media as they

continue to influence our ideas, even our values, while we obtain most of our news through unfiltered and unvetted electronic screens. The process of radicalization continues to increase the divide between Democrats and Republicans, with major channels on one side and Fox News along with recent upstarts such as Newsmax and OneAmerica News on the other. QAnon is one of the main players in encouraging engagement in what the left calls conspiracy theories, in which at least sixty million Americans believe, and which culminated in the January 6 of 2021 attack on the Capitol. Whom can we trust?

In all the crises facing us, from climate change and racial prejudice to public health issues to the hypnotic appeal of social media, there is one pervasive theme—a tyranny of trust through misinformation and disinformation—where you've decided to trust until it's pointed out that not all the information given to you is trustworthy. Let me explain.

How do we deal with the loss of trust related to all these issues? Unless we act quickly, our planet is doomed to calamitous events that will soon overwhelm so many of us. Systemic racial inequality has been with us too long, persevering throughout our culture. Some say that prejudice is human nature. Let's explore that and see if we can foster progress toward equality at a faster rate than history has allowed so far. Can we come to realize that social media are controlling our lives in ways we don't usually recognize?

> Can we trust ourselves to foster an open-minded attitude—with a degree of skepticism and critical thinking—to discover what is true?

Research by social scientists Dr. Broockman and Dr. Kala indicates that mainstream news typically leaves us biased in one direction or another rather than imbuing us with critical thinking.[14]

As one example of a resulting bias from daily news releases

of disinformation, we need look no further than Russia's media accounts of the invasion of Ukraine, resulting in a dramatic increase in approval ratings by Russians for Vladmir Putin, from 71 percent in February 2022 to 83 percent by the following month.[15] Apparently, control over the media in Russia, with its narrative of Ukrainians being the "bad guys," worked to control Russian citizens' belief system, so contrary to that of the West. President Putin even outlawed the use of the word *war* to describe his invasion, just as the government in Myanmar outlawed use of the word *coup* to cover up its own takeover. We could not but fear the that this distorted version of reality would not end up with the prospect of nuclear conflict, as the media indicated.[16]

What we need to work harder at is fortifying the need for honesty and truth-telling to keep democracy from failing when misinformation begins to prevail. According to Moira Whelan, a director at the National Democratic Institute, "Technology has brought us closer together but has also made the world a treacherous place for democracy and individual freedom." This institute puts its efforts into citizen education, monitoring of elections, and environmental governance and resilience.[17] Following the priority of avoiding nuclear conflict comes the taking care of our planet.

Despite the plethora of disinformation about changes that are affecting our planet as well as our politics, there is a science of work that spells out the reality. In *Eaarth*, Bill McKibben[18] brings loads of scientific information to guide us into the adaptation mode of coping with the new planet we've morphed into, which he calls Eaarth. In his overview of the history and likely future of changes in our planet, Tim Flannery[19] communicates to us nonscientists what we can do at this point to mitigate the challenge at hand. In *The Sixth Extinction*, Elizabeth Kolbert[20] explains the history of periods of extinction on our planet and discusses the current one due to climate change. According to Amitav Ghosh,[21] author of *The Great Derangement*, capitalism across the globe has its own role in contributing to the climate crisis. And author Naomi Klein[22] agrees in her book, *This Changes Everything*. If we reach a higher global temperature by six degrees, according to author Mike Lynas,[23] then we may be in deep doo-doo, as he describes in his book, *Six Degrees*.

Then there's an overview by Leah Stokes writing in *The Atlantic* that three-digit temperatures are becoming more and more common, like 116 degrees F in Portland, Oregon and 130 degrees F in Death Valley.[24] The droughts are having their effect as well. Lake Mead, source of water to forty million people in seven states, had shrunken dramatically, dropping a scary 170 feet, showing the chemical markings on the sides of the lake, and revealing detritus and a number of human remains.[25]

> All this while the Amazon Rainforest in Brazil was being cut down with remarkable speed, removing the all-important "lung" function of the life-source of oxygen by trees.

Some of the trees are over 500 years old—all this for the former government's choice of short-term financial gain while the future welfare of the planet was quietly ignored.[26]

Beyond that, many species of trees are dying on their own due to climbing temperatures. In the American West, the stalwart Great Basin bristlecone pines near Telescope Peak in Death Valley National Park were beginning to fail despite their legacy of living hundreds, even thousands, of years. Today, over two-thirds of the trees are dead or dying, infected by the larvae of bark beetles, small critters known as Pinyon Ips, whose population is exploding during the growing temperatures.[27] A few tree species are in danger of becoming extinct, such as the oak referred to as *Quercus tardifolia*, known for its fuzzy evergreen leaves. "It's overwhelming and almost crushing," reports Murphy Westwood, a conservationist at the Morton Arboretum in Illinois, "the stark reality of the biodiversity crisis that's on our hands."[28]

These concerns about climate warming on Earth are backed up by scientific evidence about the warming of the oceans as well. The liquid part of our planet is just as vulnerable. According to the World Meteorological Organization, this past year revealed oceans that were warmer and more acidic than ever before.[29]

In addition, research reveals that Arctic ice is melting four times faster than the models were predicting. Even worse, some areas such as the Barents Sea north of Norway and Russia are warming up even more quickly, up to seven times what had been predicted, all this contributing to the summer heat waves creating records on an ongoing basis,[30] such as Death Valley, California, reaching a record high of 127 degrees F on Sept. 2, 2022,[31] and scorching temperatures across the nation.[32]

Yet we still have scientific findings that contradict this trend. According to a very thorough study by nine scientists from the US and the UK, studying the Thwaites Glacier in West Antarctica and published in *Nature Geoscience*, glacier retreats are not necessarily recent events as the data indicate that "sustained pulses of rapid retreat have occurred at Thwaites Glacier in the past two centuries."[33]

And then there was the inevitable food catastrophe. Due to the Russia-Ukraine conflict, the price of wheat and other grains had increased quite significantly. Between the two countries, about 30 percent of the planet's need for wheat and barley was threatened due to the war. With Russia blockading the port of Odessa and Ukraine mining its waters to avoid attack, 400 million people might not be fed their usual allotment[34], unless an agreement between the two countries could be kept alive.[35]

Back in the US, conditions were no better as a drought persisted with no letup[36] and, across the world, there was fear that we'd gone beyond the irreversible tipping point[37] in this incredibly complex weather dynamic.[38] We've already raised the temperature of the planet by almost two degrees F, so it's no surprise that, according to Yadvinder Malhi, professor of ecosystem science at the University of Oxford, "there are big shifts going on in the stability of the global climate . . . we're getting more and more extremes [like in Pakistan], or drought extremes like we're seeing in Europe, China and part of North America."[39]

We're also running out of water. In many parts of the world, the issue is becoming alarming, forcing us to consider returning wastewater back into the supply chain, characterized by some as a "toilet to tap" system.[40]

On the other side of the water coin, there is the serious claim by UN Secretary-General António Guterres that "sea-level rise is a torrent of trouble," threatened by rising tides, including "access to water, food, and health care" and "key industries like agriculture, fisheries and tourism."[41]

One very troubling phenomenon, referred to as weather whiplash, involves the double whammy of drought and flooding due to torrential rainfall. The science of it is explained by the fact that droughts dry out the land, making it less able to absorb moisture when there is precipitation. The problem then becomes exacerbated when rain comes in torrents, resulting in flooding rather than as a welcome return of water to the parched earth.

This has happened in such states as Missouri (nine-inch downpour), Kentucky (torrential rains killing over three dozen people), and late-August monsoon rains following the worst megadrought in 1,200 years in Arizona, Nevada, and New Mexico. This is "yet another clear signal that the climate crisis is with us now . . . more violent and disruptive," according to Jennifer Francis of the Woodwell Climate Research Center in Massachusetts. "Climate change is affecting people directly through these various types of extreme weather events," she adds. "By connecting to people's lives, we've gained some traction in helping make climate change a more tangible concept."[42]

Thankfully, there is finally some agreement among nations on the need to take care of our planet, not only in areas of ocean claimed by nations but also in the "wild" ocean known as the high seas, consisting of over half the planet's surface. In the spring of 2023, after twenty years of frustrating discussion, the UN finally agreed on an update of the UN Convention on the Law of the Sea to protect 30 percent of the planet's waters by 2030. Known as the 30 by 30 Plan, it is a very reassuring agreement that will do the planet a world of good, so to speak.[43] A Greenpeace statement referred to it as "a monumental win for ocean protection."[44]

Let's hope for more of these "monumental wins" to protect our vulnerable planet.

ACKNOWLEDGMENTS

There are two individuals who helped make this book appear in your hands. One is my agent, Kimberley Cameron, who maintained a positive attitude despite a few dead ends that are normal in the world of publishing. She could always be counted on for encouraging words and an uplifting demeanor. The other is my editor at Koehler Books, Becky Hilliker, who is always a pleasure to work with and "gets" my perspective, from beginning to end.

Others who helped the book substantially along the way are (in alphabetical order) Martin C. Becker, a former student who rose to the role of concept fixer; Dr. Gary Botstein, who helped me explore the many options on how to express my ideas more effectively; Dr. Linda Logdberg, who went through a number of sections with an eye to greater eloquence; Goran Matkovic, whose friendly advice was always backed by his deep thought and personal research; Dr. Steve Preston, who carefully found some needs for correction, and saved me some embarrassment; Kenny Ryback, with his expertise in graphics and marketing; Maria Taro, who lovingly oversaw the formatting of the book; Leslie Van Toole, whose creative feedback that he gave added depth to some of the chapters; and Mike Wittenstein, executive consultant and founder of Storyminers, who made some ingenious suggestions which just raised this book to a higher level.

REFERENCES:

Notes for Chapter One:

1. Fishel, A.G. Common mistakes to avoid in negotiation. Washington, DC: *Association of Corporate Counsel Resource Library*, online, Jan. 7, 2015.

2. Carter, J. *Keeping Faith*. NY: Bantam, 1982, pp. 355-400.

3. Motschnig-Pitrik, R. and Barett-Lennard, G. Co-actualization: A new construct in understanding well-functioning relationships. *Journal of Humanistic Psychology, 50 (3)*, 374–398, 2010, p. 376.

4. Wright, L. *13 Days in September: The Dramatic Story of the Struggle for Peace*. NY: Vintage Books, 2015.

5. Rovere, R. Affairs of state. *New Yorker*, Oct.2, 135-141, 1978.

6. Sanger, D.E. and Broad, W.J. Biden explores talks as China builds arsenal. *The New York Times*, Nov. 29, 2021, p. 1.

7. Pamuk, H. Israel's US Arab partners close ranks on Iran, urge Palestinian talks. *Reuters*, online, March 28, 2020.

8. Barak, E. Iran is on the cusp of a bomb. *TIME*, Aug. 8-15, 2022, p. 32.

Notes for Chapter Two:

1. Rogers, C.R. and Roethlisberger, F.J. Barriers and gateways to communication. *Harvard Business Review*, online, 1952.

2. Wright, L. *13 Days in September: The Dramatic Story of the Struggle for Peace*. NY: Vintage Books, 2015.

3. Ryback, D. Humanistic psychology's impact and accomplishments. *Journal of Humanistic Psychology, 51(4)*, 415–416, 2011.

4. Reik, T. *Listening with the Third Ear.* NY: Farrar, Straus, 1998.
5. Tomaschek, N. *Systemic Coaching.* Heidelberg: Carl-Auer, 2006, p. 55.
6. Motschnig-Pitrik, R. Significant learning communities as environments for actualizing human potentials. *International Journal of Knowledge and Learning, 4 (4),* 387–397, 2008.
7. Motschnig-Pitrik, R. and Barett-Lennard, G. Co-actualization: A new construct in understanding well-functioning relationships. *Journal of Humanistic Psychology, 50 (3),* 374–398, 2010, p. 376.
8. Carter, J. *Keeping Faith.* NY: Bantam,1982, pp. 355-400.
9. Wright L. *Thirteen Days in September: The Dramatic Story of the Struggle for Peace.* NY: Vintage Books, 2015.
10. Motschnig-Pitrik, R. and Barett-Lennard, G. Co-actualization: A new construct in understanding well-functioning relationships. *Journal of Humanistic Psychology, 50 (3),* 374–398, 2010, p. 386.
11. Rovere, R. Affairs of state. *New Yorker,* 135-141, Oct.2, 1978.
12. Crowley, M. Israel cements diplomatic links to 2 Arab states. *The New York Times,* Sept. 16, 2020, p. 1.
13. Crowley, M. Israel, U.E.A. and Bahrain sign accords, with an eager Trump playing host. *The New York Times,* online, Sept. 15, 2020.
14. Brown, J.F. As ideas swirl, it pays to use your third ear. *The New York Times,* July 27, 2013.
15. Farrell, C. and Kirkpatrick, D. (producers). Jimmy Carter: Rock and Roll President. Thunder Moccasin Pictures: *CNN.* April 15, 2020.
16. Marsalis, W. Interviewed on Real Time with Bill Maher, *HBO,* Aug. 28, 2020.

17. Rogers, C.R. and Roethlisberger, F.J. Barriers and gateways to communication. (Revised.) *Harvard Business Review*, online, 1991.

18. MacFarquhar, N. Deadly message sent by drones: It's Russia and Iran vs. the West. *The New York Times*, Oct. 18, 2022, p. 1.

19. Seddon, M. and Foy. H. Vladmir Putin abandons hope of Ukraine deal and shifts to land-grab strategy. *Financial Times*, online, April 24, 2022.

20. Trump, M.L. *Too Much and Never Enough*. NY: Simon and Schuster, 2020, p. 208.

21. Goldmacher, S. and Haberman, M. Year after riot, G.O.P. is Trump's to command. *The New York Times*, Jan. 6, 2022, p. 1.

22. Feuer, A. Jan. 6 inquiry turns its focus to new group. *The New York Times*, Jan. 4, 2022, p. 1.

23. Broadwater, L. and Feuer, A. Trump rebuffed aides over loss, denying reality. *The New York Times*, June 14, 2022, p. 1.

24. Dang, S. and Culliford, E. TikTok war: How Russia's invasion of Ukraine played to social media's youngest audience. *Reuters*, online, March 7, 2022.

25. Perlez, J. Impasse at Camp David: The overview; Clinton ends deadlocked peace talks. *The New York Times*, online, July 26, 2000.

Notes for Chapter Three:

1. Harrington, O.W. Letter to psychologist Raphael H. Rhodes who offered to hypnotize Woodard if the blindness were psychological rather than physical. Aug. 15, 1946.

2. US police chief acquitted of assault on Negro. Columbia, SC: *The*

Canberra Times, Nov. 7, 1946, p. 1.

3. Gardner, M.R. Harry Truman and civil rights. *UVA NewsMakers*, online, Sept. 26, 2003.

4. Town honors an African American WWII veteran blinded in a 1946-police beating. Atlanta, Ga: *CNN.* Feb. 11, 2019.

5. Daniel, L. On Anderson 360, *CNN.* June 13, 2021.

6. Mineo, L. The scapegoating of Asian Americans. *The Harvard Gazette*, online, March 24, 2021.

7. Horowitz, D. (2021). *I Can't Breathe: How a Racial Hoax Is Killing America.* NY: Regnery, 2021.

8. Love, C. *Race Crazy: BLM, 1619, and the Progressive Racism Movement.* NY: Emancipation Books, 2021.

9. Jones, K. *How We Can Win.* NY: Henry Holt, 2022.

10. McGhee, H. *The Sum of Us What Racism Costs Everyone and How We Can Prosper Together.* NY: One World/Penguin, Random House, 2022.

11. Miles, T. *All That She Carried: The Journey of Ashley's Sack, a Black Family Keepsake.* NY: Random House, 2022.

12. Coates, L. *Just Pursuit: A Black Prosecutor's Fight for Fairness.* Simon and Schuster, 2022.

13. *Statewide Use of Force Standardization Act. Public Act 101-0652.* General Assembly, State of Illinois, July 1, 2021.

14. National Conference of State Legislatures. *Legislative Responses for Policing—State Bill Tracking Database.* Online, May 5, 2021.

15. *George Floyd Justice in Policing Act of 2020.* HR7120—116th Congress.

16. Kirkpatrick, D.D. et al. Why many police traffic stops turn deadly. *The New York Times,* online, Oct. 31, 2021.

17. Kirkpatrick, D.D. et al. Cities rethink traffic stops by the police.

The New York Times, April 15, 2022, p. 1.

18. Jones, J.M. Black, white adults' confidence diverges most on police. *Gallup,* online, Aug. 12, 2020.
19. Fausset, R. (2022). Officers in fatal shooting of Rayshard Brooks will not be charged. *The New York Times,* online, Aug. 23.
20. Hulse, C. and Karni, A. Jackson confirmed to Supreme Court as backers hail a landmark moment. *The New York Times,* April 8, 2022, p, 1.
21. Schuppe, J. et al. Memphis police's vaunted Scorpion unit under scrutiny after Tyre Nichols' death. *ABC News,* online, Jan. 26, 2023.
22. Quoted in article by Norwood, C. Ketanji Brown Jackson will be the first Black woman justice. *The 19th,* online, April 7, 2022.
23. Quoted in article by Stableford, D. Ketanji Brown Jackson on her historic confirmation to Supreme Court: 'I am the dream and the hope of the slave'. *Yahoo! News,* online, April 8, 2022.

Notes for Chapter Four:

1. Long, M. Quoted in United Kingdom: A growing backlash against masks. *The Week, 20(986),* July 31, 2020, p. 16.
2. Gessen, M. *Surviving Autocracy.* NY: Riverhead Books, 2020.
3. Bosman, J. et al. Chicago staggers anew in a torrent of looting. *The New York Times,* August 11, 2020, p. 1.
4. Householder, M. and Bauer, S. Kenosha police: 3 shot, 2 fatally during Wisconsin protests. *The New York Times,* online, Aug. 26, 2002.
5. Jones, M. Illinois teen charged with homicide in killing of two people during Kenosha protests. *Milwaukee Journal Sentinel,* Aug. 26, 2020, p. 1.
6. Helsel, P. (2021). Kenosha killing suspect Kyle Rittenhouse's bond

terms changed after bar visit. *NBC News,* online, Jan. 22, 2021.

7. Tavernise, S. and Durston, E. A. G.O.P warnings of chaos resound in Wisconsin. *The New York Times,* Aug. 27, 2020, p. 1.

8. Bosman, J. and Mervosh, S. US investigates police shooting as Kenosha boils. *The New York Times,* Aug. 27, 2020, p. 1.

9. Burns, A. and Haberman, M. Accepting bid, Trump paints Biden as unsafe. *The New York Times,* Aug. 28, 2020, p. 1.

10. Kanno-Youngs, Z. and Shear, M.D. A 'welcome' after 3 years of 'stay out'. *The New York Times,* Aug. 27, 2020, p. 1.

11. Stolberg, S. G. Questions swirl around C.D.C.'s shift on testing. *The New York Times,* Aug. 27, 2020, p. 1.

12. Hill, C. 'We must change': Biden rolls out racial equity agenda with executive orders on prison reform, xenophobia. *Yahoo! News,* online, Jan. 26, 2021.

13. Garnett, M. Investigation into NYPD response to the George Floyd protests. *New York City Dept. of Investigation.* Dec. 2020, p. 3.

14. Barker, K. et al. Reports hammer police responses to 2020 protests. *The New York Times,* March 21, 2021, p. 1.

15. Bromwich, J. E. Officials gird for ruling that may end gun law. *The New York Times,* June 7, 2022, p. 1.

16. Levin, B. et al. Anti-Asian hate crimes reported to the police. *Center for the Study of Hate and Extremism at California State University,* San Bernardino, online, April 23, 2021.

17. Shear, M. D. 'Enough,' Biden asserts, demanding law to ban assault-style weapons. *The New York Times,* online, June 3, 2022.

18. Smith, C. (2021). Stories of slavery, from those who survived it. *The Atlantic,* online, Feb. 9, 2021.

Notes for Chapter Five:

1. Thomas, H. (Exec. Producer). *Extinction: The Facts*. London, UK: BBC, 2020.

2. Nelms, S. E. et al. Marine mammal conservation. *Endangered Species Research, 44*, 291-325, 2021.

3. Schmidt, G. A. GISS Surface Temperature Analysis (v3*). Goddard Space Flight Center, Earth Sciences Division*, FL: NASA, 2021.

4. Gibbons, D. 500 scientists send letter to UN saying, "There is no climate crisis". *The Post Millenial*, online, Sept. 28, 2019.

5. Berkhout, G. et al. There Is No Climate Emergency. *European Climate Declaration*, online, Sept. 26, 2019.

6. Baker, A. A snowless future foretold on Europe's tawny slopes. *TIME*, Feb. 20, 2023, pp. 14-15.

7. Thunberg, G. *Greta Thunberg: A year to change the world*. R. Liddell and H. Thomas, producers, B-Reel Films, PBS, April 22, 2021.

8. Wogan, D. Why we know about the greenhouse gas effect. *Scientific American*, online, May 16, 2013.

9. Hansen, J. *Hearing Before the Subcommittee on Science, Technology, and Space of the Committee on Commerce, Science, and Transportation of the United States Senate*, online, June 23, 1988.

10. Xu, C. et al. Future of the human climate niche. *Proceedings of the National Academy of Sciences of the United States of America, 117(21)*, 11350-11355, 2020. p. 11350.

11. Na, E. and Li, S. Japan's famous cherry blossoms see earliest bloom in 1,200 years as climate warms. *NBC News*, online, April 1, 2021.

12. Portner, H-O. et al. *Climate Change 2022: Summary for*

Policymakers. IPCC WGII Sixth Assessment Report, pp. 4 and 35, Cambridge University Press, Cambridge, UK and New York, NY, USA, 2022.

13. Shukla, P. R. *Climate Change 2022: Mitigation of Climate Change. Contribution of Working Group III to the Sixth Assessment Report of the Intergovernmental Panel on Climate Change.* Cambridge University Press, Cambridge, UK and New York, NY, USA, 2022.

14. Plumer, B. and Zhong, R. Stopping climate change is doable, but time is short, U.N. panel warns. *The New York Times,* online, April 4, 2022.

15. Boulton, C. A. et al. Pronounced loss of Amazon rain forest resilience since the early 2000s. *Nature Climate Change,* online, March 7, 2022.

16. Stein, T. Increase in atmospheric and atmospheric methane set another record during 2021. *National Oceanic and Atmospheric Administration, US Dept. of Commerce,* online, April 7, 2022.

17. Stege, T. Quoted in: The window to adapt to climate change is 'rapidly closing,' warns the U.N. climate-science body. *TIME,* March 14-21, 2022, p. 16.

18. Yee, V. and Alami, A. In North Africa, Ukraine war strains economies weakened by pandemic. *The New York Times,* online, Feb. 25, 2022.

19. Guterres, A. Secretary-General warns of climate emergency, calling Intergovernmental Panel's report 'a file of shame', while saying leaders 'are lying', fueling flames. *United Nations press release,* April 4, 2022.

20. Kerry, J. Quoted in Dlouhy, J.A. and Wu, J. US climate envoy John Kerry puts natural gas on notice. *Bloomberg,* online, April 21, 2022.

21. Kerry, J. Quoted in Plumer, B. et al. Time is running out to avert a harrowing future, climate panel wars. *The New York Times,* online, Feb. 28, 2022.

22. Otto, F. E. L. et al. Climate change increased rainfall associated with tropical cyclones hitting highly vulnerable communities in Madagascar, Mozambique, and Malawi. *World Weather Attribution, 13(1905),* online, April 11, 2022.

23. Reed, K. A. et al. Attribution of 2020 hurricane season extreme rainfall to human-induced climate change. *Nature Communications,* online, April 12, 2022.

24. Dahlman. L. and Lindsey, R. Climate change: Ocean heat content. *Climate.gov,* online, Jan. 12, 2022.

25. Gilbert, N. Climate change will force new animal encounters—and boost viral outbreaks. *Nature,* online, April 28, 2022.

26. Singh, K. D. and Hasnat, S. Millions displaced and dozens dead in flooding in India and Bangladesh. *The New York Times,* online, May 22, 2022.

27. Bearak, M. Climate pledges fizzle as havoc looms for globe. *The New York Times,* Oct. 26, 2022, p. 1.

28. Andreoni, M. Have we hit peak greenwashing yet? *The New York Times, Climate Forward,* online, Feb. 21, 2023.

29. Deutsch, A. et al. Dutch airlines KLM sued over 'greenwashing' ads. *Reuters,* July 6, 2022.

30. Gates, B. Meet the future in this online series about climate change. *GatesNotes,* online, April 15, 2022.

31. Klein Salamon, M. If you're anxious about the climate, try this. *The New York Times,* online, May 1, 2022.

32. Meinshausen, M. et al. Realization of Paris Agreement pledges may limit warming just below 2 °C. *Nature, 604,* 304-309, 2022.

33. Tabuchi, H. Exxon scientists predicted global warming, even as company cast doubts, study finds. *The New York Times,* online, Jan. 12, 2023.

34. Martin, P. M. et al. People plant trees for utility more often than for biodiversity or carbon. *Biological Conservation, 261(109224),* 2021.

35. Bastin, J-F. et al. The global tree restoration potential. *Science, 365(6448),* 76-79, 2019.

36. Way, R. et al. Empirically grounded technology forecasts and the energy transition. *Oxford, UK, Institute for New Economic Thinking at the Oxford Martin School: INET Oxford Working Paper No. 2021-01,* 2021, p. 13.

37. Roop, H. A. Quoted in Andreoni, M. Your power as a citizen. *The New York Times, Climate Change,* online, March 24, 2023.

Notes for Chapter Six:

1. Thompson, A. Slow-motion ocean: Atlantic's circulation is weakest in 1,600 years. *Scientific American,* online, April 11, 2018 and Boers, N. (2021). Observation-based early-warning signals for a collapse of the Atlantic Meridional Overturning Circulation. *Nature Climate Change, 11,* 680-688, Aug. 5, 2021.

2. Wahlin, A. K. et al. Pathways and modification of warm water flowing beneath Thwaites Ice Shelf, West Antarctica. *Science Advances, 7(15),* online, April 9, 2021.

3. Harvey, C. These are the biggest climate questions for the new decade. *Scientific American,* online, Jan. 4, 2020.

4. Adussumilli, S. et al. Interannual variations in meltwater input to the Southern Ocean from Antarctic ice shelves. *Natural Geoscience, 13,* 616-620, 2020. p. 616.

5. Rice, D. One of the coldest places on Earth recorded its hottest temperature ever: 100.4 degrees. *USA Today,* online, June 24, 2020.

6. Smith A. B. 2020 US billion-dollar weather and climate disasters in historical context. NOAA *Climate.gov,* online, Jan. 8, 2021.

7. Gross, S. What to do about climate change and why? *Brookings, Policy* 2020, online, Oct. 15, 2019.

8. Cheng, L. et al. 2018 continues global ocean warming. *Advances in Atmospheric Sciences, 36(3),* 249-252, 2019.

9. Kolbert, E. *Under a White Sky.* NY: Crown, 2021.

10. Asian Carp Regional Coordinating Committee. *Draft Asian Control Strategy Framework.* February 2010.

11. Branch, J. and Plumer, B. A climate crossroads with 2 paths: Merely bad or truly horrific. *The New York Times,* Sept. 23, 2020. p. 1.

12. Braddock, S. et al. Relative sea-level data preclude major late Holocene ice-mass change in Pine Island Bay. *Nature Geoscience,* online, June 9, 2022.

13. Landrum, L. and Holland, M. M. Extremes become routine in an emerging new Arctic. *Nature Climate Change,* online, Sept. 14, 2020.

14. Lerer, L. and O'Connor, P. House passes climate change bill. *Politico,* online, June 28, 2009.

15. Edge, D. et al. (Producers) The Power of Big Oil. Part Two: Doubt. PBS: *Frontline,* 2022.

16. Van Beurden, B. Quoted in Worland, J. Why we can't quit oil. *TIME,* May 23, 2022, p. 46.

17. Friedman. L. Administration said to support Alaska drilling. *The New York Times,* March 12, 2023, p. 1.

18. Maclean, R. and Searcey, D. Congo to allow more oil wells in rainforests. *The New York Times,* July 25, 2022. p. 1.

19. Bittle, J. *The Great Displacement.* Simon and Schuster, 2023.

20. Plumer, B. Earth to hit critical warming threshold by early 2030s, climate panel says. *The New York Times*, online, March 20, 2023.

21. Sengupta, S. Climate forward. *The New York Times*, online, April 18, 2023.

22. Government of India press release, Ministry of Earth Sciences, online. April 16, 2023.

23. European Space Agency. Earth observation supports latest UN climate report. *Phys.Org*, online, March 21, 2023.

Notes for Chapter Seven:

1. Plumer, B. and Schwartz, J. These changes are needed amid worsening wildfires, experts say. *The New York Times*, online, Sept. 10, 2020.

2. Plumer, B. and Popovich, N. The US has a new climate goal. How does it stack up globally? *The New York Times*, online, April 23, 2021.

3. Tankersley, J. $2 trillion for 'once in generation' fix of infrastructure. *The New York Times*, April 1, 2021, p. 1.

4. Davenport, C. et al. Big bet. *The New York Times*, April 1, 2021, p. 1.

5. Friedman L. et al. Biden, calling for action, commits US to halving its climate emissions. *The New York Times*, online, April 22, 2021.

6. Koonin, S. E. *Unsettled*. Dallas, TX: BenBella Books, 2021.

7. Flavelle, C. Climate change is getting worse, E.P.A. says. Just look around. *The New York Times*, May 13, 2021, p. 1.

8. Bouckaert, S. et al. Net zero by 2050. Paris, France: *International Energy Agency*, 2021, pp. 3 and 187.

9. Birol, F. Quoted in Plumer, B. Nations must drop fossil fuels, fast, world energy body warns. *The New York Times*: Climate and Environment, online, May 18, 2021.

10. Widdershoven, C. The IEA's latest proposal is both reckless and impossible. *Oilprice.com*, online, May 18, 2021.

11. Kasakove, S. Hottest temperatures in Arizona and Nevada history are possible. *The New York Times*, online, June 14, 2021.

12. Freedman, A. Dangerous heat wave underway in West, will shatter records. *Axios*, online, June 14, 2021.

13. Welch, C. Under the heat dome. *National Geographic*, online, June 29, 2021.

14. Isai, V. and Bilefski, D. At nearly 116 degrees, heat in western Canada shatters national record. *The New York Times*, online, June 28, 2021.

15. Einhorn, C. Like in 'postapocalyptic movies': Heat wave killed marine wildlife en masse. *The New York Times*, online, July 9, 2021.

16. Fountain, H. Climate change drove western heat wave's extreme records, analysis finds. *The New York Times*, online, July 7, 2021.

17. Sengupta, S. As California dries up, farmers are forced to sell their water. *The New York Times*, June 29, 2021, p. 1.

18. Kummu, M. et al. Climate change risks pushing one-third of global food production outside the safe climatic space. *One Earth, 4(5)*, 720-729, 2021, p.720.

19. Vicedo-Cabrera, A. M. et al. The burden of heat-related mortality attributable to recent human-induced climate change. *Nature Climate Change, 11*, 492-500, 2021.

20. Eddy, M. Hundreds missing and at least 69 are dead in Western Europe flooding. *The New York Times*, online, July 15, 2021.

21. Duncombe, J. Health costs from climate soar to $820 billion. *GeoHealth*, online, May 28, 2021.

22. Falconer, R. and Freedman, A. Wildfires rage across over 1 million acres in US West and Canada. *Axios*, online, July 12, 2021.

23. Dhara, C. and Koll, R. M. How and why India's climate will change in the coming decades. *The India Forum*, online, July 23, 2021.

24. Quoted in Klein, E. It seems odd that we would just let the world burn. *The New York Times*, online, July 15, 2021.

25. Masson-Delmotte, V. et al. Climate change 2021. *Sixth Assessment Report of the Intergovernmental Panel on Climate Change*, Aug. 7, 2021.

26. Guterres, A. Secretary-General calls latest IPCC Climate Report 'Code Red for Humanity', stressing 'irrefutable' evidence of human influence. *United Nations Meetings Coverage and Press Releases*. NY: United Nations, 2021.

27. Friedman, L. et al. Climate report stressed unity but stoked ire. *The New York Times*, Aug. 10, 2021, p. 1.

28. Fischer, E. M. et al. Increasing probability of record-shattering climate extremes. *Nature Climate Change, 11*, 689-695, 2021.

29. White Oak Pastures, Bluffton, GA 39824.

30. Mozzafarian, D. et al. The carnivore's guide to cutting back. *Health and Nutrition Letter, 39(3)*, 2021, p. 6.

31. Friedman. L. and Davenport, C. Amid extreme weather, a shift among Republicans on climate change. *The New York Times*, online, Aug. 13, 2021.

32. Thunberg, G. et al. This is the world being left to us by adults. *The New York Times*, online, Aug. 19, 2021.

33. Gensler, G. Statement on ESG disclosures proposal. *US Security and Exchange Commission Statement*, online, May 25, 2022.

34. Erickson, P. et al. *The Production Gap Report*. Stockholm, Sweden: Stockholm Environment Institute, 2021.

35. Nugent, C. Temperature tantrum. *TIME*, Aug. 6-15, 2022, p. 8.

36. Kaplan, S. Inaction on climate change imperils millions of lives, doctors say. *The Washington Post*, online, Oct. 20, 2021.

37. Morrisroe, C. Senator Manchin puts pollution profits over people. *Sierra Club*, online, July 15, 2022.

38. Horowitz, J. 'We need water': A parched Europe swelters. *The New York Times*, Aug. 19, 2022, p. 1.

39. Smith, A. Britain braces for record heat, risking lives and infrastructure. *NBC News*, online, July 18, 2022.

40. Eddy, M. Germany will fire up coal plants again in an effort to save natural gas. *The New York Times*, online, June 19, 2022.

41. Davenport, C. Republican drive to tilt courts against climate action reaches a crucial moment. *The New York Times*, online, June 19, 2022.

42. Mann, C. C. New challenges for us all. *National Geographic*, 36-41, April 2020.

43. Vanderbilt, T. A rising tide lifts all grids. *TIME*, July4/July 11, 2020, 60-63.

44. Davenport, C. et al. California to ban the sale of new gasoline cars. *The New York Times*, online, Aug. 24, 2022.

45. Cochrane, E. House passes climate, tax, and health package. *The New York Times*, online, Aug. 12, 2022.

46. Watson, K. Biden signs Inflation Reduction Act into law, sealing major Democratic victory on climate, health care and taxes. *CBS News*, online, Aug. 16, 2022.

Notes for Chapter Eight:

1. Burns, A. et al. Allies of Trump start to break ranks on virus. *The New York Times,* July 20, 2020, p. 1.
2. Vlessides, M. COVID-19 'infodemic'. *Medscape,* March 27, 2020.
3. Knapp, S. et al. Therapy in the time of COVID-19. *The National Psychologist, 29(3),* 2020, p. 8.
4. Hoffman, J. Mistrust of corona virus vaccine could imperil widespread immunity. *The New York Times,* July 18, 2020, p. 1.
5. Navarro, P. Anthony Fauci has been wrong on everything I have interacted with him on. *USA Today,* July 14, 2020.
6. Siddiqui, S. US to invest more than $3 billion in COVID-19 antiviral development. *The Wall Street Journal,* online, June 17, 2021.
7. Glenza, J. The Delta variant is spreading. What does it mean for the US? *The Guardian,* online, June 16, 2021.
8. Waltz, E. COVID vaccine makers prepare for a variant worse than Delta. *Scientific American,* online, Oct. 24, 2021.
9. Bosman, J. In struggle with Omicron, the one constant is change. *The New York Times,* Jan. 10, 2022, p. 1.
10. Wheeler, S. Today's cartoon. *The NewYorker, Daily Humor,* online, March 8, 2022.
11. Stolberg, S. G. Fauci says he believes Paxlovid kept him out of the hospital, even though he tested positive again. *The New York Times,* online, June 29, 2022.

Notes for Chapter Nine:

1. Mandavilli, A. Can you get COVID again? NY: *New York Times Live,* July 22, 2020.

2. Robbiani, D. F., Gaebler, C., Muecksch, F. et al. Convergent antibody responses to SARS-CoV-2 in convalescent individuals. *Nature* https://doi.org/10.1038/s41586-020-2456-9, 2020.

3. Lin, W. W. et al. Prolonged persistence of measles virus RNA is characteristic of primary infection dynamics. *Proceedings of the National Academy of Science, 109(37),* 14989-14994, 2012.

4. Sekine, T. et al. Robust T cell immunity in convalescent individuals with asymptomatic or mild COVID-19, *Cell,* 11564, Aug. 2020.

5. Long, Q-X. Clinical and immunological assessment of asymptomatic SARS-CoV-2 infections. *Nature Medicine,* June 18. doi.org/10.1038/s41591-020-0965-6, 2020.

6. Lei, Q. et al. Antibody dynamics to SARS-CoV-2 in asymptomatic and mild COVID-19 patients. *medRxiv* 2020.07.09.20149633, 2020.

7. Thevaragan, I. (2020). Breadth of concomitant immune response underpinning viral clearance and patient recovery in a non-severe case of COVID-19. *medRxiv* 2020.02.20025841, 2020.

8. Singh, S. Coronavirus patient re-hospitalized in China's Chengdu after testing positive again. *Reuters World News,* Feb. 21, 2020.

9. Lan, L. Positive RT-PCR test results in patients recovered from COVID-19, *Journal of the American Medical Association, 323(15),* 1502-1503. Feb. 27, 2020, doi:10.1001/jama.2020.2783.

10. Xie, X., Zhong, Z., Zhao, W., Zheng, C., Wang, F. and Liu, J. Chest CT for typical corona virus disease 2019 (COVID-19) pneumonia: Relationship to negative RT-PCR testing. *Radiology.* Published online, February 12, 2020. 2020;200343, doi:10.1148/radiol.2020200343.

11. Korber B. Spike mutation pipeline reveals the emergence of a more transmissible form of SARS-CoV-2. *bioRxiv*, doi.org/10.1101/2020.04.29.069054. April 30, 2020.

12. Grifoni, A., Weiskopf, D., Ramirez, S. I. et al. Targets of T cell responses to SARS-CoV-2 coronavirus in humans with COVID-19 disease and unexposed individuals. *Cell, 181(7)*, 1489-1501, 2020.

13. Sette, A and Crotty, S. Pre-existing immunity to Sars-CoV-2. *Nature Reviews Immunology, 20*, 457-458, 2020.

14. Greenbaum, J. A. et al. Pre-existing immunity against swine-origin H1N1 influenza viruses in the general human population. *Proceedings of the National Academy of Sciences of the USA, 106*, 20365-20370, 2009.

15. Hancock, K. et al. Cross-reactive antibody responses to the 2009 pandemic H1N1 influenza virus. *New England Journal of Medicine, 361*, 1945-1952, 2009.

16. Zhao, J. et al. Airway memory CD4(+) T cells mediate protective immunity against emerging respiratory coronaviruses. *Immunity, 44*, 1379-1391, 2016.

17. Carlson, C. J. et al. (2022). Climate change increases cross-species viral transmission risk. *Nature*, online, April 28, 2022.

18. Woolery, C. Quoted in Achenbach, J. A crisis foretold—and ignored. *The Week, 20(986)*, July 31, 2020, p. 36.

19. The Bulletin. Bird flu isn't a danger to humans . . . yet. *TIME*, Feb. 27, 2023, p. 10.

Notes for Chapter Ten:

1. Woolery, C. Quoted in Achenbach, J. A crisis foretold—and ignored. *The Week, 20(986)*, July 31, 2020, p. 36.

2. Petrosillo, N. et al. COVID-19, SARS, and MERS. *Clinical Microbiology and Infection, 26(6),* 729-734, 2020.
3. Mandavilli, A. First documented corona virus reinfection reported in Hong Kong. Reported in the Corona Virus Outbreak in *The New York Times*, online, Aug. 24, 2002.
4. Tillett, R. and Sevinsky, J. et al. Genomic evidence for a case of reinfection with SARS-CoV-2, *The Lancet,* preprint, Aug. 27, 2020.
5. Yong, E. America is trapped in a pandemic spiral. *The Atlantic*, online, Sept. 9, 2020.
6. LaFraniere, S. et al. For regulators, the rock is the pandemic, the hard place is Trump. *The New York Times,* Sept. 13, 2020, p. 1.
7. Woodward, B. *Rage*. NY: Simon and Schuster, 2020.
8. Powell, A. A public-relations campaign to build trust in COVID vaccine? *The Harvard Gazette: Health and Medicine*, online, Sept 16, 2020.
9. Baker, P. Trump scorns own scientists over virus data. *The New York Times*, Sept. 17, 2020, p. 1.
10. Grady, D. and Thomas K. 2 firms share plans on trials for a vaccine. *The New York Times,* Sept. 18, 2020, p. 1.
11. Tyson, A. et al. US public now divided over whether to get COVID-19 vaccine. *Pew Research Center,* online, Sept. 17, 2020.
12. Gold, J. and McKinley, J. (2020). New York will review virus vaccines, citing politicization of process. *The New York Times,* online, Sept. 24, 2020.
13. Miller, B. L. Science Denial and COVID Conspiracy Theories: Potential Neurological Mechanisms and Possible Responses. *Journal of the American Medical Association,* online, Nov. 2, 2020.

14. Karlsson, A. C. et al. The known unknowns of T cell immunity to COVID-19. *Science Immunology, 5(53)*, online, Nov. 18, 2020.

15. Mandavilli, A. The coronavirus is staging a comeback. *The New York Times*, online, Feb. 25, 2021.

16. Greshko, M. COVID-19 will likely be with us forever. *National Geographic Science, Corona Virus Coverage*, online, Jan. 22, 2021.

17. Stolberg, G. S. et al. Enough vaccine for 'every adult' in May, Biden says. *The New York Times*, Online, March 3, 2021, p. 1.

18. Lythgoe, K. A. et al. SARS-CoV-2 within-host diversity and transmission. *Science*, online, March 21, 2021.

19. Mandavilli, A. Virus variants likely evolved inside people with weak immunity systems. *The New York Times*, online, March 15, 2021.

20. Choi, B. et al. Persistence and evolution of SARS-CoV-2 in an immunocompromised host. *New England Journal of Medicine, 383*, 2291-2293, 2020.

21. Avanzalo, V. A. et al. Case study. *Cell, 183(7)*, 1901-1912, 2020.

22. Kemp, S. A. et al. SARS-CoV-2 evolution during treatment of chronic infection. *Nature*, online, Feb. 5, 2021.

23. Park, A. Vaccines vs. viral variants. *TIME*, March 15/22, 2021, p. 12.

24. Mervosh, S. et al. 400,000 deaths in a year and failure at every level. *The New York Times*, Jan. 18, 2021, p. 1.

25. Goodman, J. D. New York's control of virus surprises experts. *The New York Times*, Aug. 18, 2020, p. 1.

26. Gamio, L. and Symonds, A. Global virus cases reach new peak, driven by India and South America, *The New York Times*, online, May 1, 2021.

27. Allen, J. et al. India Coronavirus Map and Case Count. *The New York Times,* online, May 2, 2021.

28. Bosman, J. and Mervosh, S. COVID data shows US is 'turning the corner,' fueling a sense of hope. *The New York Times*, May 6, 2021, p. 1.

29. Yamamoto, N. et al. SARS-CoV-2 infections and COVID-19 mortalities strongly correlate with *ACE1* I/D genotype. *Gene, 758,* 144944, 2020.

30. Gemmati, D. and Tisato, V. Genetic hypothesis and pharmacogenetics side of Renin-Angiotensin-System in COVID-19. *Gene, 11,* 1044, 2020.

31. Denyer, S. and Achenbach, J. Researchers ponder why covid-19 appears deadlier in the US and Europe than in Asia. *The Washington Post*, online, May 28, 2020.

32. Uria, D. Epidemiologist warns US in 'category five hurricane status' in COVID-19 pandemic. *UPI*, online, April 4, 2021.

33. Crane, E. COVID-19: New, infectious strain of Delta variant detected in the US. *New York Post*, online, Oct. 20, 2021.

34. Lander, E. S. and Sullivan, J.J. *American Pandemic Preparedness.* Washington, DC: The White House, 2021.

35. Toy, S. Antidepressant Fluvoxamine significantly reduces COVID-19 hospitalization. *The Wall Street Journal,* online, Oct. 28, 2021.

36. Mueller, B. COVID deaths at low rate even as infections climb. *The New York Times,* June 21, 2022, p. 1.

37. Wallace, J. et al. Excess death rates for Republicans and Democrats during the COVID-19 pandemic. *National Bureau of Economic Research, Cambridge MA: Working Paper 30512,* Sept. 2022, p. 2.

38. Tayag, Y. What does it mean to care about COVID anymore? Mask smarter, not harder. *The Atlantic*, online, Nov. 21, 2022.

39. Matsuyama, K. Top Pfizer and Moderna executives diverge on need for fourth COVID shot. *Bloomberg*, online, March 15, 2022.

40. Kakowski, M. Coronavirus briefing. *The New York Times*, online, March 30. 2021.

41. Weintraub, K. A COVID turns 3, experts worry where the next pandemic will come from. *USA Today*, Jan 1, 2023.

42. Goodrum, F. et al. Virology under the microscope—a call for rational discourse. *mSphere*, Jan. 26, 2023.

43. Inglesby, T. How to prepare for the next pandemic, *The New York Times, The Next Pandemic*, online, March 12, 2023.

44. Gates, B. The world needs pandemic firefighters. *The New York Times, Opinion, The Next Pandemic*, March 19, 2023.

Notes for Overview:

1. Ryback, D. *Dreams That Come True*. NY: Doubleday/Dolphin, 1988.

2. Ryback, D. *Look 10 Years Younger/Live 10 Years Longer*. Englewood Cliffs, NJ: Prentice Hall, 1995.

3. Ryback, D. *Putting Emotional Intelligence to Work*. Woburn, MA: Butterworth-Heinemann, 1998.

4. Ryback, D. *Love Sex and Passion for the Rest of Your Life*. Atlanta, GA: Humanics, 2003.

5. Ryback, D. *ConnectAbility*. NY: McGraw-Hill, 2010.

6. Ryback, D. *Secrets of a Zen Millionaire*. Melbourne, FL: Motivational Press, 2015.

7. Hulse, A. *Cries from the Deep*. Durham, NC: Lulu Press, 2015.

8. Vohra, K. et al. Global mortality from outdoor fine particle pollution generated by fossil fuel combustion: Results from *GEOS-Chem. Environmental Research, 195,* 110754, 2021.

9. Rogers, C. R. and Ryback, D. One alternative to nuclear planetary suicide. In R. F. Levant and J. M. Shlien (Eds.), *Client-Centered Therapy and the Person-Centered Approach.* NY: Praeger, 1984.

10. Perlroth, N. Microsoft says Russian hackers viewed some of its source code. *The New York Times,* online, Jan. 2, 2021.

11. Sanger, D. E. et al. As understanding of Russian hacking grows, so does alarm. *The New York Times,* online, Jan. 2, 2021.

12. Dilanian, K. et al. Russian hackers breach US government, targeting agencies, private companies. *NBC News,* online, Dec. 14, 2020.

13. Paul, C. and Matthews, M. The Russian "Firehose of Falsehood" propaganda model. *Rand Corporation,* online, April 14, 2016.

14. Broockman, D. and Kalla, J. The manifold effects of partisan media on viewers' beliefs and attitudes. *OSF Preprints,* online, April 1, 2022.

15. Hobson, P. Putin's approval rating soars since he sent troops into Ukraine—state pollster. *Reuters,* online, April 8, 2022.

16. Alter, E. 'The Day After' director addresses the prospect of a nuclear war between America and Russia: 'These are very scary times.' *Yahoo! Entertainment,* online, April 8, 2022.

17. Whelan, M. *NDI Brochure 2020.* Washington, DC: National Democratic Institute, online, Jan. 31, 2021.

18. McKibben, M. *Eaarth.* NY: St. Martin's, 2011.

19. Flannery, T. *The Weather Changers.* NY: Grove Press, 2007.

20. Kolbert, E. *The Sixth Extinction.* NY: Picador/Macmillan, 2015.

21. Ghosh, A. *The Great Derangement.* Chicago: University of Chicago Press, 2017.
22. Klein, N. *This Changes Everything.* NY: Simon and Schuster, 2015.
23. Lynas, M. *Six Degrees.* Washington, DC: National Geographic, 2008.
24. Stokes, L. C. The infrastructure bill won't cut it on climate. *The Atlantic,* online, July 14, 2021.
25. Locher, J. Withering drought shows Lake Mead boat graveyard. *Associated Press,* online, July 11, 2022.
26. Maisonnave, F. Deforestation in Brazilian Amazon hits tragic record in 2022. *Associated Press,* online, July 12, 2022.
27. Kaplan, S. Scientists rush to save 1,000-year-old trees on the brink of death, online, *The Washington Post,* July 15, 2022.
28. Kaplan, S. Saving Methuselah. *The Week,* Aug. 5, 2022, p. 37.
29. Spring, J. Oceans are hotter, higher, and more acidic, climate report warns. *Reuters,* online, May 18, 2022.
30. Fountain, H. A signal of climate change just got more dire. *The New York Times,* Aug. 12, 2022, p. 1.
31. Knowles, D. Death Valley sets record for hottest Sept. day—and California's heat wave isn't over. *Yahoo!News,* online, Sept. 2, 2022.
32. Shapero, J. Hundreds of temperature records broken as heat wave scorches the US *Axios,* online, July 25, 2022.
33. Graham, A. G. C. et al. Rapid retreat of Thwaites Glacier in the pre-satellite era. *Nature Geoscience, 15,* 706-713, 2022, p. 706.
34. Roman, A. The coming food catastrophe. *The Economist,* online, May 19, 2022.

35. Zinets, N. 'Glimmer of hope' as Ukraine grain ship leaves Odesa port. *Reuters*, online, Aug. 1, 2022.

36. O'Donnell, G. US is 'losing some of these smaller farms' amid historic drought, economist says. *Yahoo!finance*, online, Aug. 27, 2022.

37. Armstrong McKay, I. et al. Exceeding 1.5°C global warming could trigger multiple climate tipping points. *Science, 377(6611)*, online, Sept. 9, 2022.

38. Flexas, M. M. et al. Antarctic Peninsula warming triggers enhanced basal melt rates throughout West Antarctica. *Science Advances, 8(32)*, 2022.

39. Malhi, Y. Quoted in Taylor, D. B. Europe's shrinking waterways reveal treasures, and experts are worried. *The New York Times*, online, Sept. 22, 2022.

40. Shao, E. Its aquifer dwindling, Virginia finds a solution in the sewers. *The New York Times*, Oct. 21, 2022, p. 1.

41. Adler, B. UN Security Council warns of sea-level rise: 'A torrent of trouble'. *Yahoo! News*, online, Feb. 14, 2023.

42. Erdenesanaa, D. Prophet of the polar vortex. *Scienceline, Environment*, online, March 21, 2022.

43. Larson, C. and Whittle, P. Nations reach accord to protect marine life on high seas. *Associated Press*, online, March 5, 2023.

44. Einhorn, C. Nations agree on language for historic treaty to protect ocean life. *The New York Times*, online, March 4, 2023.

45. Ramirez-Feldman, L. What to know about XBB.1.16, a new Omicron variant on the W.H.O.'s radar. *Yahoo!News*, online, April 18, 2023.